BILDUNG

BILDUNG
KEEP GROWING

by
Lene Rachel Andersen

NORDIC
BILDUNG

Bildung – Keep Growing
© Lene Rachel Andersen & Nordic Bildung, 2020
www.nordicbildung.org

ISBN: 978-87-93791-08-4
E-book ISBN: 978-87-93791-10-7
Design: Ulla Holger, Petit Bureau, and Lene Rachel Andersen
Print: Scandinavian Book

Danish version ISBN: 978-87-93791-09-1
Danish e-book ISBN: 978-87-93791-11-4

FOREWORD

By the co-presidents of the Club of Rome

The publication *Bildung - Keep Growing* by Lene Rachel Andersen has been accepted as a Report to the Club of Rome. This book is a thoughtful and thought-provoking guide to enable humanity to re-focus on what is essential and to understand life-long learning, education and thinking as a unifying force. It is rich in comparisons between the phases of Developmental Psychology and Bildung as a complex interplay between individual development, learning and collective culture. Importantly, this book has a regional, European narrative but a global ambition.

Bildung is here presented as a tool for personal development into a self-authoring stage that enables one to function as a confident responsible citizen able to express unique individuality within a shared cultural value system. Lene Rachel Andersen makes a bold foray into proposing the concept of the Bildung Rose to represent unity in diversity and nesting humanity in nature, of which we are a part.

A better understanding of the power of Bildung as a unifying force is essential as humanity exits COVID-19 and as we need to build greater resilience and solidarity in community evolution as we prepare for future pandemics and crises. The concepts of Bildung, Circles of Belonging and the Bildung Rose promote the possibility for a new brand of national identity which is centered on a holistic approach to the "self", "peoplehood" and "community." An identity built around a compassionate pride of belonging that is accepting of all cultures and thinking rather than today's brand of extremist nationalism or populism.

Bildung - Keep Growing is of high relevance to everybody thinking seriously about knowledge exchange, education and life-long learning as anchors for holistic economic and political development at the community, national and global levels.

Reports to the Club of Rome do not necessarily represent the opinion of the Club of Rome as an organization, nor the opinion of all its members. The acceptance as a Report to the Club of Rome indicates that the Club of Rome appreciates and promotes the publication as an important intellectual contribution.

Sandrine Dixson-Declève   Mamphela Ramphele
Co-President, the Club of Rome   Co-President, the Club of Rome

EXECUTIVE SUMMARY

Bildung is moral and emotional maturity. Bildung is also to have the education and knowledge necessary to thrive in your society; bildung is to be deeply embedded in culture and community while having the autonomy to carve your own path in life. Bildung is always personal and unique.

Bildung is a German word that has no word in English. Beginning in the 1770s, German philosophers explored bildung as a secular form of inner development and it became popular among the bourgeoisie.

In Denmark, a pastor realized in the 1830s that the peasants needed bildung too, and he envisioned a new kind of school: the folk-high-school. In 1851, a Danish teacher, Christen Kold, figured out how to teach in such a way that young farmhands learned to think for themselves: he told them moving stories and let them ask questions. Once he had their attention, he could teach them new farming techniques, science, philosophy, history, religion, literature, art, economic theory, and political science.

Norway, Sweden and Finland copied the folk-high-school concept in the 1860s and by 1900, a critical mass of youngsters in the Nordic countries had upgraded their skills and their thinking, and the Nordics had gone from being among the poorest countries in Europe to being among the richest. This development and the bildung that carried it also meant that the Nordics made the transition from agricultural feudal societies to modern, democratic, industrialized nation-states peacefully.

As we are facing new challenges from digitization, globalization, a pandemic and environmental changes we need bildung for the 21st century and the book concludes by exploring what that might look like.

PREFACE

Humanity at a crossroads

Atman, a Sanskrit word, means inner self, spirit or soul, and breath. *At-men*, a German word, means to breathe. The connection between the two words is not a coincidence; both have the same Proto-Indo-European root. Danish is an Indo-European language too, a Germanic language in fact, and in Danish, to breathe is *ånde,* while spirit is *ånd.* The Hebrew word *ruach* means wind, breath, or spirit, and when the Bible opens by telling that God's spirit sweeps over the water, it is *ruach.* When God threatens to kill all life on Earth in a flood, it is the *ruach* of all life that is to disappear. Later in the Bible, *ruach* comes to mean the individual human soul, mind, or consciousness, that which is of higher awareness than mere instinct, that which can contemplate and serve God.

It is perhaps no big wonder that breath, spirit, and consciousness are connected in the spiritual traditions and in different languages. After all, our consciousness and life itself are what disappear when our breathing stops.

It is a diabolic irony that through our very breath, humanity is now connected. Not through wisdom of the spirit, but through a virus; not through life, but through the risk of death.

While we have created technologies and economic infrastructures that connect us around the globe, we forgot to upgrade our understanding, our consciousness, our sense of responsibility, and our consciense; our spirit. We forgot to study, learn, and teach to everybody that which is at the core and the forefront of human knowledge. We forgot to think, and we forgot to understand ourselves as connected around the globe and to protect life. We also forgot to see ourselves as a part of nature and to pay heed to the spiritual traditions that, different as they are, all tell us to treat Earth's resources with humility and respect. We were poor stewards of the Earth we inherited; we are poor gardeners.

Sufficient knowledge to understand your circumstances, the emotional maturity to act appropriately in time, and the cultivation to express how and why are all summed up in one German word: *Bildung*.

To solve the existential crises we are facing as a species, such as climate change, mass extinction of species, surveillance capitalism, artificial intelligence (AI), terrorism, skyrocketing inequality, and financial collapses—and pandemics such as the COVID-19—we need bildung, and we need it at a massive scale and fast.

We are the first generation to experience a global disaster unfold within months, and be able to watch it unfold globally in real time. We are also the last generation who can claim we had no clue. We are the generation that will be defining the future for all of humanity. It is our political and technological choices that will define the climate, the wellbeing of eco-systems and the technological infrastructure of coming generations. We have their quality of life, their prosperity, and their level of freedom in our hands. It is our responsibility. If we choose to implement constant surveillance everywhere in order to regulate people's behavior, we will have forced it upon coming generations; if we choose not to implement constant surveillance, we will have given coming generations the same freedom, responsibility, and choice: to take away freedom from future generations or to keep it. Similarly with nature: if we destroy it, we hand that destroyed planet over to coming generations; if we save it, we hand over the responsibility.

Instead of robbing everybody of their freedom, responsibility, and a green planet, we can mature. We can see ourselves as an integral part of nature, and we can become responsible. We can promote bildung.

To introduce and explore bildung, and to suggest a path forward towards a wiser and green planet, this book is comprised of five parts:

- The human spirit; what makes life meaningful?
- Meaning-making and bildung: emotional development and the society in which it takes place.
- How Denmark turned bildung into folk-bildung, exported it to the other Nordic countries, and how this changed the Nordics.
- More and better bildung; a better understanding, framing what happened, and making it operational in the 21st century.
- Some personal reflections on the wider implications of bildung.

Bildung is an elusive phenomenon, and I do not suggest that by reading this book, you will have a manual to start a program or a new school, but I am certain that you will have a new foundation for understanding our potential as individuals and as a species. I also hope the book will inspire you to start a conversation about better education, bildung, and the potential of the human spirit wherever you are.

With this book, I hope to reach those who are interested in the future of humanity and the wellbeing of our planet. I write with policymakers and the curious and conscientious citizen in mind, and I aim to write in plain language though I often use very abstract and academic concepts. If we are to solve the major crises that we are facing, writing different books for academics and everybody else will not foster a meaningful conversation among us. Facing the gigantic paradigm shift that is necessary if we are to hand over a habitable planet to our children and grandchildren, we need shared frames of reference.[1]

There is no need to try to hide that I am writing from a European perspective, but I have done my best not to make the book too Eurocentric. However, since the topic of the book originated in Europe, it is hard to avoid.

---

1   Speaking of references: In order to increase readability, footnotes and references have been kept to an absolute minimum. There is a literature list at the end of the book and, since the first half of the book is based on *The Nordic Secret - A European Story of Beauty and Freedom* (Fri Tanke, 2017), there is an online collection of sources by topic, which can be found on the website of that book: https://www.nordicsecret.org/sources-by-chapter/

I am also writing from a Danish perspective; I am Danish and was born and raised in Denmark. In my late 20s, I went to the US several times; I went there as a Dane and returned as a European. There are aspects of Denmark that I hate so much that sometimes I just feel like yelling at my country. Our appreciation of mediocracy, for instance, and the ever-present "*hygge*," which became "Word of the Year 2016," but which is really just a way of dying without living first.

On the other hand, I have to admit: Denmark has it pretty much figured out. In international surveys, the Danes are the happiest and have low corruption and the highest levels of trust in other people and in public institutions, and Denmark is amongst the top countries for business.

As my Swedish colleague, Tomas Björkman, and I explored in our book *The Nordic Secret*, the secret behind Denmark and the other Nordic countries is: bildung.

Thank yous

Two people, in particular, have contributed to this book. My colleague Tomas Björkman with whom I wrote *The Nordic Secret – A European Story of Beauty and Freedom* (Fri Tanke, 2017); many of the core insights from that book are also in this book. My colleague Mette Hvid Brockmann with whom I work every day at Nordic bildung and who is also my editor. There is no need to be melodramatic, but I could not have written this book without you.

This book has also benefitted tremendously from comments and input from Stefan Bergheim, Sturla Bjerkaker, Bo Heimann, Gregg Henriques, Christer Nylander, Zak Stein, Ane Storgaard, and Ernst von Weizäcker. Thank you all for your feedback.

Lene Rachel Andersen,
Copenhagen, May 2020

Food for thought

When was the last time you made somebody grow?

How did that feel?

THE HUMAN SPIRIT

Making life meaningful

Why are we here?

And now that we are, what should we make of it?

The first question has intrigued humans, probably for as long as there have been humans around. Every culture on Earth, including the smallest and least technologically advanced hunter-gatherer tribes, have creation myths explaining how the world was created and why. The second question is rather new, because throughout the majority of human history, the struggle for survival was occupying everybody, and what to make of life was rather obvious: survive and make sure your children do too!

Today, at least in the wealthy West, both questions hit us differently.

To some, the first question has a religious answer: God put us here, and life came with obligations and moral value. To others, the question has a rather bleak answer: DNA emerged, mutated, and evolved to build cells around itself. Cells evolved into multicellular life, vertebrates, primates, and eventually humans; life has no intrinsic value; we just happen to be here because previous generations reproduced well and survived successfully. If there is to be any deeper meaning to life, we must create it ourselves. Which leads us to the second question:

What to make of life? Once survival has been taken care of, what's the point? We find perhaps the oldest known struggle with this existential emptiness in Ecclesiastes: "Utter futility!—said Koheleth—Utter futility! All is futile!" and then it goes downhill from there... 2,500-year-old nihilism in the face of life's meaninglessness. In other words, if life is to be meaningful, we have to make it so!

With productivity as high as it is in the most technologically advanced societies, we are about to find ourselves in the existentially awkward situation that we are no longer necessary for our own survival. Hypothetically, robots could produce everything. Life is thus in our own hands now, much necessity is gone, and it is up to us to make it meaningful, find a purpose, do what is important and fulfilling, and engage ourselves in what makes us thrive and feel lasting meaning and joy.

There are two major obstacles to this: our inner world and personal choices, and the outer world that defines a number of circumstances over which the individual has little or no control.

We, therefore, need to see ourselves both as individuals with autonomy and as beings, who are integral to and embedded in something bigger, be it family, community, country, or the globe as a whole. That we are integral to a community or system means that even though we may feel that we are in no control, we still contribute to there being the community or the system. Without our being in it, the community or system would be different. Maybe just a tiny bit, but still different.

This double existence, as both autonomous and integral, can be weaker or stronger.

We can be so lacking autonomy that the only truly individual aspect of our life is our bodily functions; this is the condition of the newborn, but it is also the fate of the concentration camp prisoner.

Detachment from others may mean that we are not an integral part of any family or community. If this deprivation happens in early childhood, few develop properly. Later, we can be so lacking connectedness to others that we have no meaningful or true relationships at all; it is possible to be so emotionally, culturally, and morally detached from others that we despair. This may happen due to tragic personal loss, but it may also be the fate of the individual in a concentration camp or authoritarian system where no personal relationships or autonomy are allowed. Under these circumstances, existence is neither autonomous nor integral to human life; it is rather the absence of both.

In some respects, this loneliness and detachment from others, from culture, from shared morality, norms, and emotions, is what we have done to ourselves, to our societies, and our educational systems in the postmodern West. Liberalism and capitalism at their best set people free and create wealth; at their worst and with no correction from tradition and morality, they pit us against each other and break down the social fabric and our symbolic worlds. Schools that are reduced to PISA and other tests, to measurable indicators, to constant competition, and to "teaching factories" producing nothing but a competitive workforce are starving the human soul. They are detaching children and young adults from that which makes life worth living. Autonomy is squelched; attachment does not fit into a spreadsheet.

The far more meaningful, rich, fulfilling, and fun alternative is, of course, high degrees of both autonomy and integration. Upbringing, schools, communities, and societies that develop that which is unique in each child, that create strong social bonds, and that foster independence and connectedness to both people, culture, and society, provide scaffolding for meaningful growth. Likewise, meaningful is the adult life in which we have the ability to be in charge of our own life-situation, where we can seek and access information freely and express ourselves. A life of autonomy and integration is a life where we are free to enjoy the arts and aesthetics of our own and other cultures, their richness and depth, to provide for ourselves in the surrounding economy, to study and learn, to develop a moral and ethical backbone and the ability to speak up for oneself and on behalf of others, to know our 'place' in history and have a sense of rootedness in the collective journey of our country and of humankind. To be empowered and active as a citizen, to engage in the organization of one's society. It is deep integration into the social fabric, which provides all those enriching elements in one's life. It is freedom, obligations, independence, interdependence, and responsibilities at the same time. Furthermore, it is bildung.

About bildung

There is no English word for *Bildung*, so the German original will have to do. (You pronounce it *bild-ung;* the *'ung'* part with the same short 'oo' as in the name of the Swiss psychologist Jung.) It comes from the word *Bild*, which means image, and originally referred to forming oneself in the image of God or Christ. In the mid-1700s, it became a secular phenomenon, and the *Bild* one was aiming for, was the personal image of one's fully developed self. It was the German Idealist philosophers of the late Enlightenment and the early Romantic era, such as Johann Gottfreid Herder, Friedrich Schiller, and G.W.F. Hegel, who explored this kind of secular bildung in the decades around 1800.

Bild-ung is thus both a formation process and the result of a formation process. The reason for not just using the English word *formation*, is that bildung comes with a rich philosophical tradition.

Bildung represents a complexity that makes it hard to fully grasp. Even to Germans who, for the past couple of generations, have reduced the word to mean no more than education in the most ordinary sense of the word: the school stuff that can be measured in a test.

About the book and our opportunities

Because bildung is both a foreign word in the English language and an elusive concept, this book has several goals:

- To briefly trace the Greek, Czech, Swiss, French, Scottish, and British roots of the otherwise very German concept of bildung, and to thus show that bildung is an aspect of the European heritage that we have forgotten.
- To explore the concept of bildung and present it to people outside the Germanic tradition.
- To re-introduce it into the German vernacular in its original, complex sense.

- To share how the Danes transformed bildung into folk-bild-ung in the 1800s and laid the foundation for the success of the Nordic countries.
- To show that bildung is an essential human phenomenon that we overlook at our own peril, but which points towards a better future.

As these lines are written, it is still too early to say what even the short-term outcome of the COVID-19 virus and the lockdown will be, but one lesson already learned is this: when governments really want something, they can find the money to pay for it.

Folk-bildung may be the best way to restore our societies and their economies in the aftermath of the pandemic.

Every human being has the potential for autonomy and deep integration, the capacity for emancipation and responsibility; everybody has the potential and deserves access to bildung. That ought to be our overall political endeavor.

Food for thought

When was the last time you changed your mind on a political issue? What did you fear the most: Being wrong after you changed your mind or looking silly?

BILDUNG & EMOTIONAL DEVELOPMENT

Philosophy vs. psychology

So, what is bildung actually? There is an overlap between bildung philosophy and modern developmental psychology, but they also differ. Modern developmental psychology works in a clear-cut manner and is useful when we want do describe emotional development scientifically. Bildung is elusive but grasps the complex interplay between individual development, learning, and collective culture. By comparing bildung philosophy and developmental psychology, we can explore how advanced the understanding of the human psyche was more than 200 years ago, and how advanced the thinking was behind the Western educational systems when they were created. It also shows us that the foundation of political freedom and democracy is the emotional development of the citizens.

Most people are aware that our psyche, our emotions, and our moral capacity change during childhood and into adulthood. What people are generally less aware of is that this development continues in our adult years. Yet, whenever you point out to people that there is usually a significant difference between the average 35-year-old and the average 75-year-old when it comes to their emotional life and how they approach the world, nobody seems to be surprised. This maturation is adult emotional development, psychological development, personal development, self-development, or ego-development; it has many names. It is also bildung.

Psychology and ego-development

According to developmental psychology, as we mature, we go through bigger and smaller transitions and transformations, some of which can be very frustrating, if not downright painful. The general pattern regarding this development is that once we are 'on the other side' of a transition in our development, when we have transformed, we do not go back.

Several psychologists have developed descriptions of these phases in life; some present five phases, others 13 or anywhere in between. The first psychologist to approach our mind like this was the American psychologist James Mark Baldwin (1861-1934), but the most famous is probably the Swiss child psychologist Jean Piaget (1896-1990), who was inspired by Baldwin. Piaget explored the emotional development in children until around age 15, and among his insights is that the mind, i.e., our meaning making, can best be understood as an evolving organism. As we encounter the world, our assumptions about it are either confirmed or need to be revised. As we keep revising our assumptions, we learn and grow.

An American psychologist who took inspiration from Piaget and looked at moral development, not just in childhood, but throughout life was Lawrence Kohlberg (1927-1987). In the 1960s, he suggested six levels of moral reasoning, which in their shortest form look like this:

1. Obedience and avoiding punishment: Will I get caught?
2. Instrumental and oriented towards self-interest: Does this serve me?
3. Oriented towards interpersonal relations and conformity: Will they like me and trust me?
4. Oriented towards authority and maintaining social order: Will this serve societal structures?
5. Oriented towards the social contract in general: Does this serve everybody and the bigger picture?
6. Oriented towards universal ethical principles: Does this serve a purpose beyond our own time?

As already mentioned: once we have entered a new phase in life, we do not go back. This means that from a later phase or level of morality, the earlier phases look immature or immoral. If my moral reasoning orients me towards maintaining social order (Kohlberg 4), people with a moral orientation towards "Does this serve me?" (Kohlberg 2) seem immoral.

Robert Kegan's 5 orders of mental complexity

One of today's simplest models regarding adult emotional development was developed by Robert Kegan (b. 1946), professor of adult learning and professional development at Harvard Business School.

With just five phases, each phase is broader and it is easier for us to relate to the phases if we are not trained psychologists. The fact that the categories are so broad also makes it less problematic to look at what kind of development is valued and promoted in groups and entire societies; the broader the categories, the bigger tolerance for individual variation within each category.

To have or to be had
– increasing self-control and sense of being a subject

A central part of Kegan's model of ego-development is the understanding that what controls us at one stage in life can become an object of our control later in life. When we develop this extra control and responsibility over ourselves, our freedom increases, and so does our perception of being a subject in the world.

A concrete example is the baby who cannot yet control her bowel movements; hence, we provide her with diapers. The bowel instincts 'have the child,' so to speak, but as she grows and the sense of self begins to emerge, this changes. The baby does not have an aware sense of self, but around the age of two, the toddler begins to perceive herself in the world; there is 'Me.' This Me discovers that 'it' has a body, and by taking control over that body, the *self*, the *subject* or *ego* emerges and makes the body an object to that subject. Once the instincts do not have the child anymore, but the child-subject has them, can control them, and takes responsibility for them, i.e., does not need a diaper, the child experiences a new degree of freedom.

This process of being in the throes of something, transcending it, and taking possession of it goes on through life. When the child is around age 4, we want the subject in the child to be able to see her impulses and emotions as 'objects.' Instead of just crying or being angry, we increasingly want her to be able to say "I am sad" or "I am angry" and deal with the emotion as something she has. Where the toddler and the small child was had by impulses and emotions, the older child transcends the impulses, *has* emotions, and becomes free to deal with them.

As the older child and teenager transcends the emotions and comes to have them as an object, he or she is instead embedded in the norms of family and society. The teenager is in the process of stepping out of the existential nest of the parents and of becoming an adult who is 'had' by the norms that are shared in society. The subject learns to see her own emotions as objects through the norms of society; in our teen years, we make society's norms about emotions our own norms about our emotions.

As we mature, we can experience personal conflicts with the collective norms, and as we do so, we can come to see these collective norms as objects as well. One can transcend the norms of society subjectively, develop one's personal opinion about them, hold them as objects, and decide for oneself what to do with them. Should one conform or make personal life choices?

There is thus a pattern in the way the ego or sense of self evolves: what 'is' or 'has' the subject at one phase in life can become the object to a more complex subject, ego, or sense of self later. Our consciousness, our sense of freedom regarding ourselves and our sense of responsibility increase each time we make such a transition, and this is what emotional or ego-development is about.

The five orders of ego-development

Kegan's model of ego-development has five "orders of mental complexity," as he calls them:

1. Early childhood (self-discovering mind)
2. Childhood (self-consolidating mind)
3. Socialized mind (self-governing mind)
4. Self-authoring mind
5. Self-transforming mind

Between each two orders of ego-development, there is a phase of transition until the individual has settled into the new consciousness. Like Kohlberg's levels, these phases of ego-development evolve in a given order; once our mind has developed in a certain way, we won't go back. Unless we are under dire stress or the like.

Early childhood – 1st order of mental complexity
– self-discovering mind

Early childhood, according to Kegan, is the period from 2 to 6 years of age. At this age, the child has a sense of self, but lacks impulse control and cannot delay gratification. She also does not recognize that other people have their own point of view or purposes; if she feels something, she assumes that others feel it too. She has a magical and animistic worldview and cannot grasp the relation between cause and effect, which means that she cannot tell stories as a series of connected events: the princess with the golden shoe is suddenly Superman on a horse, which is also a car.

Psychologists have a number of names for this phase in life; in *The Nordic Secret,* we decided to call this phase **self-discovering**.

Transition out of early childhood – mental complexity 1½

From around age 5, the surrounding adults can demand impulse control. Often to the child's great frustration, but eventually, she will master it.

Childhood – 2nd order of mental complexity
– self-consolidating mind

From around the age of 6, the child has figured out cause and effect, and stories become narrative sequences that we as adults perceive as stories, not just stuff jumbled together. This sense of ordered narrative is closely related to her own sense of self and how she now perceives the world as consistent over time; there is a before, a now and an after; and me is the same me living through all of them. This means that choices now have consequences to the future me; "if I cheat now, they won't play with me tomorrow."

Gradually, the big child understands that others have their own point of view, and she has hers; she can also take the role of another person and can manipulate others on behalf of her own goals. Playing 'Shop' with other children during the self-discovering phase (2-6 years) was one of those games contributing to developing this ability.

She can keep appointments and live up to obligations and expectations if adults set the terms, and she becomes increasingly capable of putting such obligations above her own needs here and now if they serve her longer-term self-interests. What she cannot do is to construct the obligations herself.

Psychologists have different names for this phase; in *The Nordic Secret,* we called it **self-consolidating**; this is the age when the child begins to identify enduring qualities about herself, such as "I'm good at drawing and really like pizza, but I don't like eggs." In order to get a stable sense of self, it is important that the surroundings recognize her own perception of herself and support it while she is also learning to play by common rules, be it social norms or very concrete rules such as those in sports or board games. Part of her self-consolidation happens among peers; from around the age of 5, moral guidance increasingly comes from peers rather than from parents.

Transition from childhood to socialized mind
– mental complexity 2½

From her tween and early teen years, the child increasingly meets demands of responsibility, mutuality, and expectations that she keeps her promises. We expect trustworthiness and that she begins to behave according to the shared norms, even when nobody is watching. Learning to govern oneself is a stressful phase, though.

Socialized, self-governing mind
– 3rd order of mental complexity

As we go through puberty, an emotional realm opens inside us that allows us to have intimate relationships in a new way. We can connect with other people at a deeper level, be it with friends or sexually and emotionally with a partner/spouse. The intimacy and the pain whenever somebody breaks the trust in such deep relationships force us to take a new kind of responsibility for our own behavior and to live up to the expectations of others. We develop a new capacity for empathy and for sharing at an internal level rather than merely seeing social interchanges as transactions. Increasingly, we can internalize another person's emotions and point of view and see the world from that person's perspective. We enjoy shared experiences, feelings, and moods.

This new realm of intimacy also allows for a deep sense of connectedness to God, art, country, or certain ideals. This allows us to feel a sense of duty and develop a capacity for collaborative self-sacrifice in groups where we share a history and a narrative such as our religion and/or nation. Being loyal to friends' and family members' feelings becomes of the highest moral value; the same goes for any of our other in-groups, be it a soccer team, religion, or nation.

What happens is that we find moral scaffolding in our in-groups, and these groups provide us with identity, and this has consequences. With a socialized mind, threats to my in-groups feel like an existential threat to Me. As self-governing, socialized teens or adults, we tend to construct the world in "us vs. them" terms between those who scaffold and support me and those who probably do not and therefore pose a threat.

Given our group dependence as self-governing, we tend to see our ideology and/or religion as *the Truth*, and we get our identity from these Truths. They are absolute Truths, and we identify with them in a way that does not leave room for accepting truths and moral values from non-agreeing groups; "you think differently" most often means to us "you are wrong."

Kegan's 3rd order matches Kohlberg's 3rd level: "Will they like me and trust me?" As self-governing, we cannot mentally put ourselves morally outside the group and its norms. They have us.

Transition from self-governing to self-authoring mind – mental complexity 3½

Since we are not always happy with everybody else's expectations, frustration can set in. If the norms are against, say, divorce, but one's marriage is horrible, one may reach the point where personal wellbeing beats the norms. Frustration can become so strong that we want to move beyond the norms and redefine our life.

Developing beyond the self-governing, socialized mind is an individual process and highly personal. Since this is about allowing our true self to emerge, despite the expectations of others, there may not be anybody in the surroundings who fully understands what it is we need; they may be self-governing according to the very norms we are struggling to transcend, and there may not be anybody who can support our personal journey. This is particularly the case in traditional societies where conformity is a shared norm; in modern, highly individualistic societies, we expect people to 'find themselves,' but it may be hard nevertheless.

Typically, the transition from the socialized, self-governing mind to the self-authoring mind happens in connection to a personal, social crisis such as the death of a parent, a divorce or losing one's job. Something changes so profoundly in one's life that ignoring it is not an option, and one needs to make an existential choice.

Self-authoring mind – 4ᵗʰ order of mental complexity

The self-authoring individual, according to Kegan, seeks self-realization and is capable of viewing the norms and truths of society as objects, among other objects. As self-authoring, we are capable of setting ourselves emotionally or intellectually outside of society's general perspectives and of taking a personal stand, even if it means being rejected by family or friends. We gain autonomy.

We, of course, still enjoy intimate personal relationships and belonging to groups, but it must be morally principled and honest. Principles have higher authority than the emotions of the people in the in-group and of any group as such; family, nation, fellow congregants, and spiritual leaders are not ultimate authorities any more; I am. I am personally responsible for judging (or misjudging) whether something is right or wrong and will serve the societal structure or not (Kohlberg 4).

Transition from self-authoring to self-transforming 4½

When we are truly self-authoring, the drive for personal success may mean that we accept norms and rules if these allow us to thrive and grow, but when this is no longer enough, we want the world around us to grow too. Things that don't serve a higher purpose seem shallow, and maybe one's response is an ironical distance, perhaps even to oneself. Stage 4½ may thus be called **self-distancing** because we want to connect to more than just our own agendas and ambitions.

Self-transforming mind – 5ᵗʰ order of mental complexity
– a systems perspective

This stage of ego-development is the hardest to describe, but many grandparents know it, at least within the family. It is the ability to see not just how other people and their interactions affect everybody individually and as a group, but also how one's own actions, attitudes, and idiosyncrasies affect everybody and the totality.

Having put one's own children into this world and having tried to raise them well, one has made a number of mistakes. Now, these children are raising their own children, and are now making many of the same mistakes. Wisdom is the ability to see the dynamics among family members and knowing which mistakes to interfere with and which to stay out of.

If we develop this kind of systems perspective on bigger groups such as community or nation, this 5th order of mental complexity becomes a complex mode of being where no truths or principles are absolute, and people, situations, and principles are seen as interrelated. As a 'global grandparent' or 'self-transformer' with a systems perspective, one comes to accept, if not enjoy, paradox. With a systems perspective like this, the self is a part of an interconnected whole.

Self-transforming may come across as an unstable state, but there is still a sense of personal continuity. The self still has the same memories, skills and tendencies that connect the self over time. This mode of being, though, only emerges with sufficient crises, losses, and pushbacks, and in due time.

The five orders of complexity

Summing it all up, Kegan's five orders of mental complexity look like this:

1st Order	2nd Order	3rd order
Age 2 to 6	Age 6 to teen	Teen and adult
Self-discovering*	Self-consolidating*	Self-governing
• The child needs authority outside and boundaries; cannot keep agreements • First peers • Jumbled thinking • The child is had by her impulses	• Child needs authority outside and boundaries; can keep agreements • Searches for group • Structured thinking • The child is had by her emotions	• Internalized norms and boundaries • Conformity • Puts group above principles (and self) • The individual is had by the group's norms, ideals, and values

Table 1: Ego-development

The development process

There is a common denominator in the processes of going from one phase of life to the next: there is a sense of surrender in order to acquire more freedom. It is an emotional and philosophical paradox, but whenever we are ready to surrender our current sense of self to the next and take upon ourselves a new degree of responsibility, we also acquire a new degree of freedom.

When our body 'surrendered' to our mind, and we accepted being in control of our body, we gained the freedom to listen to our emotions. When our emotions surrendered to the norms of our society, and we accepted these norms as our own, we gained the freedom to engage intimately with others because we could be trusted; by containing ourselves emotionally, we could develop new emotional experiences. As our socialized self and the social norms are overruled by personal frustration, we can acquire autonomy. At each stage of development, there is a surrender and an opening of new realms, and the inner turmoil that we feel during such phases of transition is the struggle between two levels of responsibility and freedom.

4th order	5th order
Adults	Adults
Self-authoring	Self-transforming
• Own norms • Has ideals and values • Puts principles above group • The person is had by personal autonomy and cannot let go	• Mutuality • Renewing norms • Systems perspective / sees full picture incl. self • Holistic thinking • Sees the process and accepts the flow

* Not Kegan's words

Epistemology

Before we move on to exploring bildung, I would like to introduce the term epistemology. Kegan, at some point, calls the five phases epistemologies, but that is not how I am going to use the word.

When I use the word epistemology in the following, I refer to the language, symbols, culture, and knowledge through which one is able to understand the world and thereby that, which (along with one's ego-development) defines how one perceives the world. The epistemology is a set of culture-colored glasses through which one sees the world.

I am going to use the term, particularly when I talk about collective epistemology and cultural development. We each have our individual epistemology that is constantly being updated and (hopefully) improved as we live and learn, and then there is the collective cultural, societal epistemology. Any functioning society has an epistemology that is shared by the majority of the population: a shared language, shared knowledge, shared assumptions. There are individual variations, of course, but the shared epistemology allows us to understand together.

Bildung and German philosophers

The earliest concept of bildung, *paideia*, emerged in ancient Greece, so this idea has deep European roots. The bildung philosophers we are going to explore now typically did not refer back to paideia, though, their bildung philosophies grew from frustrations in and with their own society.

It was a society very different from ours, and there are a couple of reasons for bringing the historical context into the exploration of bildung. The first reason is to highlight the connection between personal, societal, cultural, and political development: as individuals, we grow in or are inhibited by a context, and only if we do grow can we change the world around us for the better: more freedom, more responsibility. The second reason is to show how much effort went into creating the freedoms we enjoy in the West today, and how important philosophy and thinking are as historical factors. Intellectuals are crucial for everybody's wellbeing, and societies without philosophers and freedom of thought and speech suffer poverty and oppression. The third reason is that people 250 years ago, or for that matter even earlier, were not dumb; the best minds, who enjoyed intellectual freedom and good peer groups, developed profound insights that are still crucial today.

Whenever we look at history, we have a tendency to look at it from our current perspective, and our judgment of our ancestors is, therefore, rarely very favorable to them. Their moral values and political decisions seem less cultivated, if not downright primitive. It was not our ancestors, who had limited intellectual capacity, though; it is very often ourselves, because we do not understand them and their time.

If, instead of looking back at history, we come into the historical development in the same order as events unfolded, we get a much better understanding of why people thought and acted the way they did. Hence, in order to get the best possible understanding of when, where, how, and why, the concept of bildung emerged and what huge consequences it had and still has for us today, we begin our journey a little bit earlier than when the actual bildung philosophy emerged:

Europe in the 1600s

The early 1600s was the era of the Counter Reformation and the Thirty Years' War (1618-1648), during which Catholics and Protestants fought over the power structure in Europe.

During those years, a Czech pedagogue, Comenius (1592-1670), came up with several principles regarding how to best teach children. Among his insights was that education must build on what the child already understands, otherwise the content will be meaningless. Many rulers in Europe, among them the King of Sweden, hired Comenius as a school consultant, and he had a huge influence on the creation of the early school systems in Europe; he has been called the father of modern education.

This was a feudal Europe, which meant that everybody was born into what can best be described as a caste in society. With minor variations across Europe, the feudal system had three estates: clergy, aristocracy and commoners, and above everybody was the ruler, be that a king or a count (plus, in Catholic areas, the Pope). Clergy was the first estate and the most privileged, second was the aristocracy, and the rest were commoners. Nobody socialized or married across estate boundaries, and there was practically no way anybody could work himself out of the estate into which he was born, except the sons of the aristocracy and, in some cases, sons of burghers who could study theology and become clergy. The commoners' status varied from place to place, but many in effect lived in slavery and with no access to education what so ever. In Catholic Europe, women of the aristocracy—and to some extent, the bourgeoisie—could become nuns, but besides that, women were married off within their estate.

An emerging exception was the upper level of the third estate, the burghers or bourgeoisie who had certain rights and privileges in the ring-walled cities of the time. Rights and privileges that non-burgher-commoners did not enjoy. Among these burghers, the successful became a 'middle class' that was sometimes very wealthy, educated, and did not really fit into the age-old feudal structure of obligations and privileges. They were the artisans and merchants who profited in the First Industrial Revolution and the capitalism that emerged in the 1400s, and which included Gutenberg's invention of printing with movable type. By around 1700, this middle class had laid the foundation for the modern capitalist economy. Some burghers had worked themselves up to considerable economic power, but political power was still with the ruler, the clergy and the aristocracy, and in Catholic Europe, with the Pope.

The Enlightenment, Pietism, and pubs

The latter half of the 1600s was the era of Isaac Newton (1643-1727) and the emerging Enlightenment with both scientific and technological breakthroughs. One of these breakthroughs was the steam engine, which was invented in 1698 and became the defining factor of The Second Industrial Revolution. Investments in this new means of production—and in the colonies, the plantations and the associated slave trade—came from the aristrocracy and the bourgeoisie, the latter who then, of course, became even richer but also more self-aware as a political class.

As their material riches expanded, their intellectual hunger grew as well. If Gutenberg's printing press from the 1440s was the communication technology that boosted the Renaissance and sparked the Reformation, then newspapers and encyclopedias were the new sources of information and the communication technologies that sparked the Enlightenment. In continental Europe, the milieus around the encyclopedias were cultural salons, generally hosted by women, where—very unusual for the time—progressive members of the aristocracy and the bourgeoisie met on equal terms. This was a radical breakdown of the social barriers between the second and third estate. In the UK, 'public houses' or 'pubs' were the new kind of meeting place: men went there to read newspapers and to discuss important matters. A common denominator between the salons and the pubs, though, was that political discussions were not tolerated by the rulers, so people had to be careful regarding what topics to discuss. Generally, science, the arts, the exploration (and exploitation) of the globe, and trade (including the slave trade) were safe topics.

Parallel to this rational and cerebral wave of the Enlightenment, in the late 1600s, there was a hunger for spirituality and the passion of the heart. In the Protestant areas, this craving found its expression in Pietism, a strand of Christianity, which focused on the personal faith and circumvention of the believer. This was new. Until Pietism, Christianity, to most Europeans, was more like water to the fish: it was a circumstance. Pietism called for a deep, inner conversion, and a personal passion for Christ; he was the image, the *Bild*, according to which one shaped one's inner being. Outer signs of prosperity were shunned; instead, the Pious donned black and simple clothes and lived for their connection to the divine, their salvation, and their *bildung*. To the modern spectator, they look bleak and dark, but their reality was different: they felt a deep and new kind of personal emotional life. How rich and beautiful this felt to them is illustrated by the fact that Pietism is what Johann Sebastian Bach

(1685-1750) expressed in his music; some of his pieces are even called 'passions.'

So, as we enter the 1700s, there are three very strong cultural waves defining Europe: a colonizing and industrializing capitalism, an intellectual, cerebral Enlightenment, and a deep, passionate, protestant, Christian spirituality of the heart, Pietism.

Formation and bildung

The first philosopher to focus on the inner development from a secular point of view was the Third Earl of Shaftesbury (1671-1713). Around 1700, he wrote about formation: an emotional and moral development that produced three different kinds of beauty.

The first kind of beauty is beautiful things and beautiful people with not too much going on in their minds; they look good but have no significant thoughts, perform no important deeds, and have no moral compass. The second kind of beauty is the people who copy other people who do beautiful deeds, and the third kind of beauty is the moral people who do the beautiful deeds out of their own accord and whom others copy. The way Shaftesbury described these three kinds of people and their beauty very much resembles Kegan's phases 2, 3, and 4: self-consolidating, self-governing, and self-authoring.

Throughout the 1700s, Shaftesbury was read and discussed among philosophers and authors on the European continent, and by mid-century, so was David Hume (1711-1776).

Hume explored his own mind: what is the mind when it is and is not thinking? His philosophy is, in some respects, close to the Buddhist tradition of noticing your thoughts as they pass through your mind, but until Hume, the process of the mind itself had not been explored in Europe.

On the continent, before 1760, two poets particularly stood out with regards to the 'bildung movement' that was about to emerge: Friedrich Gottlieb Klopstock (1724-1803) and Christoph Martin Wieland (1733-1813). Both were mystics and wrote Christian poetry that satisfied the spiritual hunger. Klopstock is particularly interesting because he wrote a poem called *Frühlingsfeyer / Celebration of Spring*, and this poem was read among the German bourgeoisie as a call for a political spring. The German thinkers are not known for political thinking, so it is interesting that poetry was interpreted politically. Wieland is interesting because he was the first to translate the French word *Éducation* into the German word *Bildung*, and by that using (for the first time), *Bildung* as a secular concept that did not relate to the image of God or Christ.

In other words: between 1700 and 1760, there was an emerging awareness in Europe of what goes on in the mind; European thinkers were directing their focus away from God and Christ and towards our own inner workings.

Rousseau, Émile and the emotions

The big paradigm shift among intellectuals in Europe came in 1762 with Jean-Jacque Rousseau's book *Émile, ou de l'éducation / Émile, or on Education* (actually: upbringing).

Rousseau (1712-1778) was originally from Switzerland, then moved to Paris, then moved back again, was expelled and put under censorship, moved in with David Hume, ended up in a horrible conflict with Hume, moved around some more, and generally lived a chaotic life. He never married but fathered five children with his mistress, all of whom he forced her to give up to an orphanage since he did not consider himself fit to be a father. Yet he wrote perhaps the most influential book about child development ever.

In 1762, when Rousseau was around 50 years old, he produced two works that made him one of Europe's most important thinkers. The first was *Du Contrat Social / On the Social Contract,* about political freedom and the need for the people to rule over themselves. The opening line is famous:

Man is born free, and everywhere he is in chains.

Rousseau's second publication in 1762 was his 500-page opus on the upbringing of the boy Émile and how Émile's emotions evolved with his age. It became a Copernican turn in the European understanding of childhood, human emotions, and human existence. By 1762, the Enlightenment had starved the European civilization of its emotional aspects, and *Émile* landed like rain on dry land. Suddenly, what many were sensing was described, and if one wanted to be a philosopher, an author, or an intellectual of any kind, one could not *not* read Rousseau!

A common topic in Rousseau's writings was the conflict between our emotions and the norms of society. The feudal system, general oppression, distorted expectations, and religion did not allow people to develop as emotionally healthy and morally responsible individuals nor to live their life to the fullest.

What is particularly interesting from a bildung point of view is that the way Rousseau described the mental and emotional development of the boy Émile completely matches a modern child and developmental psychology. What Piaget wrote in the 1920s and Kegan and others write today, is in complete concordance with Rousseau's descriptions from 200 years earlier in a completely different society and culture. The education or upbringing that Rousseau suggested definitely has its flaws (among other things, the boy does not have any peers, just his adult mentor, and not really any other relationships either), but the understanding of the maturation of the child and his mind, and the correlation between his physical and mental development still matches children today. Among the radical new ideas proposed by Rosseau was that the child's emotions and curiosity should direct the learning, not the ambitions of the teacher; Rousseau turned pedagogy and education upside down.

For all its flaws, it was a book that changed Western civilization, and the way the French word *éducation* is explained throughout the book, it is obviously much more than what we usually consider education. It is bildung.

German Bildung

Among the German philosophers who read Shaftesbury, Rousseau etc., and who began to write about different stages of moral and emotional development, different stages of autonomy or freedom, were quite a few. The most important are: Immanuel Kant (1724-1804), Gotthold Ephraim Lessing (1729-1781), Moses Mendelssohn (1729-1786), Thomas Abbt (1738-1766), Johann Gottfried Herder (1744-1803), Johann Wolfgang Goethe (1749-1832), Friedrich Schiller (1759-1805), Johann Gottlieb Fichte (1762-1814), Wilhelm von Humboldt (1767-1835), Georg Wilhelm Friedrich Hegel (1770-1831), and Friedrich Wilhelm Joseph Schelling (1775-1854). And in Switzerland, Johann Heinrich Pestalozzi (1746-1827).

I am not going to explore all of them, but will focus on Herder, Goethe, and Schiller, who were not just authors, poets, playwrights, and thinkers; they were angry young men fighting for freedom with the pen! They were also promoted by a woman: Duchess Anna-Amalia von Sachsen-Weimar-Eisenach (1739-1807), who changed the course of European history by her political agenda. We are also going to take a brief look at Kant, Mendelssohn and Pestalozzi.

Herder & Goethe

At age 17 in 1762, Herder took up theology studies and philosophy in Königsberg, which is today Kaliningrad in Russia. His professor was 38-year-old Immanuel Kant, who had not made a name for himself as a philosopher yet. Young Herder was very bright, completed his studies in just three years, and at 20 years old landed himself a job as a high-school teacher and preacher at the main cathedral in Riga, Latvia. He was a huge fan of the poet Klopstock and the philosopher Thomas Abbt, and while in Riga, he wrote a number of essays and books, one of them about Abbt and his philosophy.

By 1769, Herder was getting bored with Riga and wanted to see the world; to make a long story short, he ended up in Strasbourg in the summer of 1770. There were two reasons, in particular, he decided to stay in Strasbourg: he had fallen in love with a girl not far from there, and Strasbourg had a very famous surgeon, Dr. Lobstein, who could fix an eye problem for him. The surgery took place in the operating theater of the medical school with students watching, and after the operation, Herder needed somebody to help him. A 21-year-old student volunteered. The student was not a medical student, though, but a law student who had read some of Herder's books, and volunteering gave him a chance to meet Herder and talk to him.

The name of the law student was Johann Wolfgang Goethe, and for two weeks in October 1770, Herder and Goethe hung out together and talked about Shakespeare, German folklore, Ossian (a collection of Gaelic folklore poems), Shaftesbury, Klopstock, Rousseau, Wieland, Lessing, and many others. Very likely, they discussed more than that. They were young men who were frustrated with their prospects in the strongly hierarchical feudal society.

The reason it is fair to guess that they also talked about societal issues, perhaps even political issues, is that in 1773, a book came out, which they had written together with legal scholar and social theorist Justus Möser (1720-1794): *Von Deutscher Art und Kunst, einige fliegende Blätter / About German Essence and Arts, some Flying Letters.* It has been called a *Sturm und Drang* manifesto. In the book, they discuss big emotions, and what it means to be a people and share a cultural heritage, they compare the poetry of Ossian and Shakespeare to the Icelandic Eddas, and the passions of the Celtic and Norse mythologies, and they explore cultural development. Towards the end of the book, they write:

> The human race is destined to a progression of scenarios, of bildung, of manners.

In other words: cultures evolve over time, and humans develop morally and emotionally too.

Here, in 1773, Herder, Goethe and Möser were laying the foundation for German Idealism and Romanticism—to which we shall return shortly.

Herder's and Goethe's big individual breakthroughs, however, were in 1774 when they set the course for their individual authorships, i.e. their self-authorship as well as their writing authorship.

Herder; bildung and peoplehood

In the book *Auch eine Philosophie der Geschichte zur Bildung der Menschheit / Another Philosophy of History Concerning the Development [bildung] of Mankind,* Herder connects the personal bildung of the individual to the bildung of the civilizations or peoples to which the individuals belong. This is not bildung in the image of God or Christ; Herder's concept of bildung is secular, and he introduces a new way of understanding the importance of culture in a people and to the individual. Throughout the book, he explores the concept of a common spirit, a *Geist,* and the culture that connects a nation or people and how, over the course of history, cultures have matured. This is by no means politically correct by today's standards, as he likens the culture of nomadic patriarchs in the ancient Orient to the bildung of early childhood and the Egyptian agricultural civilization to the bildung of childhood. The Phoenicians are tradesmen and bilded like an older child, while the Greeks are teenagers, the Romans are of a man's age, brave and noble, and the Christians in the form of Catholics are somewhat more mature; the Protestants (Herder was a Protestant) are the adults.

Herder's descriptions of bildung / maturity / psychology / ego-development at the different ages (early childhood to adulthood) are very precise, even in a modern context; it matches what Piaget, Kegan, and others say today. The characterizations of the historical civilizations, on the other hand, which are supposed to match these age groups, are problematic. Herder does not distinguish between the norms of a society and how individuals cope with them. If, for instance, a nomadic society prescribes childlike obedience to the patriarch, does that mean that, say, the patriarch's mother thinks he is wiser than she, or may she have developed an independent, adult, self-transforming mindset as a grandparent and see a bigger and deeper perspective than her son? Did Abraham toddle around in the Bible, or were both he and Sarah self-governing or self-authoring adults in a time of different expectations?

Herder's main point, though, is that all ages from early childhood to adulthood and from prehistoric nomads to German Protestants are bilded at some level, and there is a global development towards increased bildung. The drivers for this are the laws of nature, the order of the Kingdom of God, and the rules of beauty—a concept inspired by Shaftesbury. The progressing bildung is thus according to God's plan, but it is not in the image of Christ.

According to Herder, we must evolve, and when the pre-historic nomads were bilded at what Herder sees as a childhood level, it was not due to inferiority on their part but purely a matter of what was possible given the historical circumstances. It would not have been possible for an individual to develop beyond the collective stage of bildung at the time. Herder thus implies that any given culture poses some limits as well as some encouragements to the development of the individuals in that culture.

Herder's thinking regarding people, peoplehood and bildung continues over the years, and his thoughts are a crucial element in today's sense of national belonging and nationalism, i.e., the fact that as (a) people, we create a shared identity through culture. At the time, this concept of feeling connected as a people through a shared culture and not divided into feudal estates was new. A strange fact is that Jews had identified as a people through a shared culture, language and practice across great geographical distances for two millennia, and the German philosophers could identify the Jews as a people from the outside, but they were only about to discover the concept of peoplehood from the inside.

In the beginning, it was only people like Herder, Goethe, and others towards the top of German and other European societies who felt that cultural connection and belonging; it was not widespread throughout the population. What brought this sense of peoplehood about was not least the emergence of newspapers, which created a shared awareness across distances. But reading newspapers and being able to identify culture as a phenomenon, i.e. 'seeing' culture as a thing in itself and knowing that you have it, rather than just *living* a culture was not common outside the very top of society. Folklore may have been among the peasants, but they had no awareness regarding the fact that they had their lore; they were embedded in it and it in them. Abbt wrote about patriotism, and

Rousseau hinted at a sense of patriotism in *Émile*, but there is no sense of peoplehood and emotional connection in any of those books in any way similar to how Herder wrote about it.

In 1774, though, the same year Herder's book came out, Rousseau wrote *Considérations sur le gouvernement de Pologne / Considerations on the Government of Poland*, and the essay is about how to create a sense of peoplehood; an emotional connectedness throughout a people. The tool he suggested was big, majestic 'sporting' events that could stir shared emotions—a suggestion that has led some to give freedom loving Rousseau the dubious honor of inventing fascism. What he invented was nationalism, and though he wrote his *Considérations* the same year as Herder wrote about bildung of nation and individual, Rousseau's text was not published until 1782.

What binds a people together, according to Herder, is *Geist,* a spirit. The way Herder wrote about it, it is hard to tell if this spirit is supposed to be a metaphysical essence in its own right, or it is no more than a lived and practiced culture and the emotions attached to this. In 1778, Herder explored the poetry of different cultures and wrote:

> A poet is the creator of the nation around him, he gives them
> a world to see and has their souls in his hand to lead them to
> that world.

The collective bildung is thus connected to the poets and the way they express the collective culture, the collective spirit, or *Geist*.

Goethe – Mr. Youth Revolt

In 1771, Goethe passed his bar exam, he got a job, and he fell in love. The young lady married somebody else, Goethe did not like working as a lawyer, and he was trapped in the feudal order. He was not happy!

Goethe wanted to be a writer, and in 1773 he wrote his first play: *Götz von Berlichingen,* about a noble highwayman who fights the conventions of society. Götz' fight is futile, though, and eventually, he concludes that freedom exists only in the hereafter; this world is a prison. The drama struck a nerve with contemporary audiences and brought Goethe to the public's attention.

The next year, in 1774, Goethe had his big breakthrough with *Die Leiden des jungen Werthers / The Sorrows of Young Werther;* Goethe became a superstar overnight! It is a semi-autobiographical letter novel about heartbreak and the suffocating norms of society; the novel ends with young Werther committing suicide.

The novel reflected the emotions and frustrations of a generation of young people, particularly young men, and it was an immediate blockbuster. It also caused a wave of suicides among young men who identified with Werther, and the novel was banned in many, if not most, places.

Werther is stuck in a society that expects internalization of the norms and self-governance, and which does not allow him to make any mistakes; a claustrophobic self-governing phase 3 based on 'one failure and you're out!' Goethe was personally stuck in the same phase 3 society, but instead of killing himself, he wrote and literally self-authored into self-authoring phase 4. This was not enough for him, though; he wanted a society that allowed and called for the same self-authoring in everybody.

Suddenly he got a very hands-on chance to make some of those changes.

Weimar is a city a little under 300 kilometers south-west of Berlin. In the late 1700s, it had about 6,000 inhabitants and was the capital of the duchy Sachsen-Weimar-Eisenach, which also included the university town, Jena, about 25 kilometers east of Weimar. Ruling the duchy in the 1760s and 1770s was Anna Amalia von Sachsen-Weimar-Eisenach. She had been a widow since she was 19, and before her husband Ernst Augustus II von Sachsen-Weimar-Eisenach died at age 20, he had transferred the regency of the duchy to her and made her the guardian of their two sons until they reached the legal age of majority. Besides being a ruling duchess through her 20s and 30s, she was also a patron of the arts and a composer, and she deliberately wanted to make Jena and Weimar a hotspot for culture and academia. When her boys reached school age, she hired the poet Wieland as their teacher.

In 1775, the young Duke Karl August von Sachsen-Weimar-Eisenach turned 18, took over the duchy, and continued Anna-Amalia's political project. One of his first moves was to invite author and jurist Goethe to Weimar and offer him a position as *Geheimerad*, a member of the Duke's three-member cabinet. Goethe accepted, and at age 26, he joined the council on June 11, 1776.

This kind of political position was quite the accomplishment for a member of the third estate, and faced with the task of boosting culture and *bildung* in the duchy, Goethe brought in 32-year-old Herder as the new General Superintendent with responsibility for education and the head preacher at the royal church.

What is enlightenment?

When a culture goes through a major change of epistemology, i.e., a transition regarding what can be described, thought and expressed, people may not always be aware of it while it is happening. They may be aware that something is going on, but they cannot pinpoint what it is. Only later can we tell what changed and give the before and the after a name, such as the medieval era and the Renaissance.

Around 1780, the Enlightenment had been going on for around 100 years, and in December of 1783, a footnote in the magazine *Berlinische Monatsschrift* asked,"*Was ist Aufklärung?*" – What is Enlightenment? The word, or perhaps just the meaning of it, was unfamiliar.

At least two people wrote an essay giving an answer: the Jewish philosopher Moses Mendelssohn and Immanuel Kant.

Mendelssohn's essay was published in the September 1784 issue, and stated:

> The words *Enlightenment, Culture, Bildung* are new words in our language. So far, they have belonged only to book-language, the common crowd barely understands them. (...) bildung, culture,

and enlightenment are modifications made by social life; effects of the diligence and efforts of humans to improve their sociable condition.

In other words, to contemporary Germans, these concepts of enlightenment, culture, and bildung were still unclear. Yet, they somehow belonged together.

Kant had not seen Mendelsohn's answer when he wrote his own essay, which is today a classic: *Was ist Aufklärung? / What is Enlightenment?* His interpretation was different:

Enlightenment is when people leave their self-imposed minority. Minority is the inability to use one's reason without guidance from others. Self-imposed is this minority when its cause is not lack of reason, but lack of decision and courage to use one's reason without being led by others. *Sapere aude!* Dare to think! Have courage to use your own reason! is thus the motto of the Enlightenment.

Here, Kant presents enlightenment, not as a cultural era, but as something much closer to ego-development. In modern terminology, what Kant defines as enlightenment is to make the transition from self-governing phase 3 to self-authoring phase 4.

Friedrich Schiller – Mr. Punk

Like Goethe, Friedrich Schiller became a superstar almost overnight at a very young age. When he was 21 in 1781, his play *Die Räuber / The Robbers* opened in Bergheim, and it too was about the constraining conditions for young people under feudal rule: A group of angry young men turn their back on society, move to the forest and become highway men. Like *Werther* inspired a wave of suicides, *Die Räuber* inspired a wave of young men seeking freedom in the forests.

In July 1787, after having established himself as a poet and playwright, Schiller moved to Jena and became part of the intellectual milieu there.

In 1789, the French Revolution broke out, and it sent shockwaves across Europe. Among the royalty, church, and aristocracy, the news was received with horror; among the bourgeoisie, particularly among the young men, it sparked great hope: Finally, a revolution toppled a monarchy in Europe! Soon, though, as news about the bloodbath followed, the Revolution lost its glory and popularity. In fact, it turned into a great disillusion. How could the French overthrow the tyrant and then become tyrants themselves? Why such a bloodbath?

Particularly Schiller was appalled. How could humans become such beasts? Why did they not understand their responsibility under this new kind of freedom? Why could they not handle the freedom? What could it be inside humans that did not allow them to handle themselves once the authoritarian rule and its structures were gone?

In 1793-94, Schiller explored this human shortcoming philosophically in a letter correspondence, and in 1795-96 his thoughts were published as *Über die ästhetische Erziehung des Menschen, in einer Reihe von Briefen / On the Aesthetic Education [Upbringing] of Man, a series of letters.*

Basically, what Schiller says is that there are three kinds of people, which also entails three phases of human development, and between each two phases there is aesthetic education or "upbringing" – or beauty:

- First kind of people: **The savage, emotional, physical person, person of nature;** the way Schiller describes it, this person matches self-consolidating; Kegan's phase 2,
    - Upbringing 1: **Calming beauty**, aligning the emotions with society.
- Second kind of people: **The barbarian, rational person** dominated by rules and fashion, a person of artifice; matches self-governing; Kegan's phase 3,
    - Upbringing 2: **Invigorating beauty**, waking people up, making them feel their own emotions
- Third kind of people: **The *gebildet* and moral person** with a personality; matches self-authoring, Kegan's phase 4.

Beauty or aesthetics thus come in two forms: as a pacifier and as an invigorator. Neither form of change through aesthetics is a passive process, though: one must be *willing* to be open to the change and the personal transformation.

What is so interesting about Schiller's *Letters* is that the purpose is 'meta-political;' the *Letters* are explicitly about the inner transformation and bildung that must take place in people if they are to be able to handle political freedom. The *Letters* are exploring the self-consciousness and moral responsibility that people need to have if they are to have political influence. Schiller also states very clearly that as humans, we must evolve, not just individually but collectively. That is the only path to freedom, be it political or otherwise. Driven by the physical/emotional or by the rational "drive" as Schiller calls it, individuals are not free. Only as moral, reflective, *gebilded* personas, have we emancipated ourselves and can evolve *ad infinitum.*

Equally interesting is Schiller's focus on beauty and the role of beauty. Aesthetics works like pulling the rug away from under our feet and letting us fall until we decide to flap our wings and fly. But before the rug can be pulled, we also need to have an idea that there is something higher up to which we can fly, and if we are to be more than just serving ourselves, we must be willing to make a moral judgment on behalf of humanity—from the 23rd Letter:

It is thus one of the most important tasks of culture to subjugate the human, also as early as in his purely physical state, to form, and to make him aesthetic to the extent that the realm of beauty allows, because only from the aesthetic, but not from the physical state, can the moral state develop. If a human being is to have, in each individual situation, the ability to judge and the willpower to judge on behalf of the species, he must find the exit from his limited existence to an unlimited one, he must be able to make the transition from any dependent condition to independence and freedom, it must be made so that in no moment is he just an individual and serves his nature only. If he is to be suited and able to pull himself up from the circle of natural purposes to purposes of reason, then inside the first he must have trained for the latter and must already have conducted his physical disposition with a certain freedom and spirit that is according to the laws of beauty.

If we are to translate this into political philosophy, what Schiller says is that people in Kegan's ego-development phases 2 and 3, i.e., self-consolidating and self-governing, are not capable of political responsibility because they are run by either their own emotions or other people's fashion and cannot form their own independent opinion. This also corresponds with Kohlberg's levels 2 and 3: "Does this serve me?" and "Will they like me and trust me?" People whose moral reasoning only concerns benefits to themselves or whether they are liked do not have the maturity needed for political freedom and responsibility. The only people with the moral habitus not to turn political freedom into a bloodbath are the self-authoring and the self-transforming, i.e., people in Kegan's phases 4 and 5 and Kohlberg's 4, 5 and 6. Between Kegan's phases 2 and 3, there is a transition phase 2½, and according to Schiller, aesthetics can align our emotions with the norms and standards of society; through art, music, literature, etc. beauty makes us calm down and become responsible team players. Between Kegan's phases self-governing 3 and self-authoring 4, there is a transition phase 3½; according to Schiller, here beauty can wake us up, transform us and make us morally self-authoring i.e., morally responsible persons who develop an individual moral compass. What Schiller says in the last sentence in the quote above is that in order for the individual to be able to do this, he must be prepared for it. It is hard to imagine this preparedness to be gained by anything other than proper education and embeddedness in culture.

What is interesting from a historical perspective is that originally, the *Letters* were a correspondence that took place between Schiller and the Danish minister of finance, Ernst Schimmelmann, and his circle of friends, which included the sister of the Danish Crown Prince Regent i.e., royalty and top aristocrats in Denmark were in on this thinking. Schiller's ideas, of course, on the one hand, confirmed to them that sharing the political power with an uneducated populace was a really bad idea, but also, on the other hand, opened their minds to the importance of good education. We shall return to them in a moment.

Pestalozzi – Mr. Social Justice

Johann Heinrich Pestalozzi grew up in deep poverty in Zürich, and at age 17 in 1763, he started studying law because he wanted to change society and improve the conditions of the poor. At the university, he met the many new ideas of the Enlightenment, not least the political and pedagogical ideas of Rousseau (*Émile* came out in 1762).

Pestalozzi never completed his law studies though, but decided that he wanted to change the world through improved agriculture and education. He, therefore, moved in with a farmer in order to learn how to run a farm. At age 23, in 1769, he married 30-year-old Anna Schulthess; they bought their own farm and wanted to run it based on the latest agricultural science. Their plan was to then take in poor children and teach them a trade, so they could help on the farm and eventually be skilled enough to find work and make a decent living. In 1770, the Pestalozzis had a son. They named him Jean-Jacques after Rousseau and decided to bring him up according to the principles lined out in *Émile*.

All of it turned out to be one fiasco after the other. The neighboring farmers didn't get Pestalozzi's new farming ideas and sent their animals to pasture in his fields. The free education with room and board, which the couple created for the poor children, was just exploited by the children's parents who took home their children as soon as they knew enough to make money for their parents. Several times the Pestalozzis were facing bankruptcy, and raising little Jean-Jacques Pestalozzi as Rousseau had prescribed just turned out to be a disaster.

Eventually, Pestalozzi realized (his wife probably had quite the say in that realization) that there must be some level of obedience in a child's bildung, otherwise the child just becomes unruly and spoiled, which does not serve the child. Pestalozzi also learned a thing or two from taking in the many children, and over the years, Pestalozzi developed his own philosophy of pedagogy. This combined the education of *Herz, Kopf und Hand,* Heart, Head and Hand, as he expressed it: bildung must contain moral judgment, education for the mind, and practical skills; the entire person must develop.

While occupied with the many practical tasks, Pestalozzi also considered the bigger picture; the moral values of society and how the economy worked. In 1781, he wrote the first part of a novel, *Lienhard und Gertrud,* about the connection between politics, economics, and morals; the other three parts of the novel were published in 1783, 1785 and 1787, respectively. The story takes place in a small village ridden by corruption and misery, and explores the community's moral recovery. The novel became a bestseller, even far outside the Swiss cantons, and Pestalozzi soon understood that he was onto something if he wrote in a popular form.

Along with Comenius and Rousseau, Pestalozzi is considered the father of modern pedagogy and children's education, not least due to his many books.

By 1797, Pestalozzi was also thinking beyond child development and published *Meine Nachforschungen über den Gang der Natur in der Entwicklung des Menschengeschlechts / My Enquiries into the Course of Nature in the development of the Human Species.* In this book, Pestalozzi focuses entirely on adult development and describes three phases of adult maturity: the animalistic condition, the societal condition, and the moral condition. The societal condition he also calls *Bürgerliche Bildung,* civic bildung. These phases very much overlap with Schiller's emotional, rational, and moral condition and with Kegan's phases 2, 3 and 4, respectively; Pestalozzi sums it up as:

By the work of my nature, I am physical power, an animal.
By the work of my family, I am social power, skill.
By the work of myself, I am moral power, virtue.

Contrary to Rousseau, Pestalozzi emphasized *Unterwerfung,* and *Beherrschung,* subjugation, and control: one develops through the sub-jugation of the animalistic self. Pestalozzi saw the transformation from the animalistic condition (self-consolidating) to the societal condition (self-governing) as a process of enjoying increasing benefits and comfort and giving up some freedoms for the rule of law. From the societal condi-tion (self-governing) to the moral condition (self-authoring), he considers the transformation an act of will:

> I can live as an animal, a burgher or a moral human being; I can travel on the highway of animal depravity; I can confirm the lim-its of burgherly independence as defined by society's law, and finally I can elevate myself to recognition of all the errors of my animal nature and all the wrongdoing of my social hardening.

In the moral condition, Pestalozzi says, man aims to refine himself and to be of good use to his surroundings.

Idealism, Romanticism, and Nationalism

In the 1780s and 1790s, with its relative freedom thanks to Anna-Amalia von Sachsen-Weimar-Eisenach, Jena was the hothouse of German think-ing. Three major aspects of the modern world emerged there: Romanti-cism, Idealism, and Nationalism.

Romanticism has its roots in the *Sturm und Drang* that began with Herder and Goethe in 1773 and 1774. It is an antithesis to the rationality of the Enlightenment with its emphasis on folklore, emotions, spirituality, and the way we can connect with nature, be it her awesome grandeur or her silence and beauty. As culture was brought to people's attention, nature became a phenomenon as well.

Idealism was made possible by Kant when, in the 1780s, inspired by Hume, he explored how we co-create our perception of the world: there is the real world out there and the ideal world in our mind. The 'ideal' world does not mean a perfect world, but the inner world that our mind creates (ideal = idea). According to Kant, we only have access to our representations of the world, the idea(l) in our mind, not to the real world out there. Our mental construct is made up of the combination of our mental *a priori* organizing abilities, such as the ability to distinguish between before vs. after, and the inputs we get from the real world. All we can ever encounter is that mental construct made up of *a priori* organizing plus input.

Since our mental models of the world are what allow us to interact with the world and hence modify it, our interaction with the real world is loops upon loops of inputs, mental constructs (ideals), and actions. Idealism thus sees matter and spirit, nature and man, humanity, and the individual as interconnected and as making up a whole interconnected system with emergent properties. The real world thus has spirit.

What is tricky, though, is the German word for spirit: *Geist*. It is used in German for mind as well as spirit, and there is always a choice of how to translate *Geist* into English. In German, even today, a number of academic fields such as theology, philosophy, psychology, history, linguistics, sociology, etc. go under the name *Geisteswissenschaften* (sciences of the spirit). Therefore, when the German Idealists spoke of *Geist*, we have to figure out if they meant a supernatural mind with its own consciousness, or a spirit, which could be purely symbolic as in 'we held the meeting in a friendly spirit,' which does not mean that we were accompanied by any extra consciousness.

Idealism (with a capital I) in the philosophical sense means that mind and matter are interacting in the same process, and that ideas, through our actions, are changing the world. By that understanding, we get close to our current everyday use of the word idealism (not with a capital I): we have some high thoughts or goals regarding the world, and we want to change it accordingly.

The **Nationalism** that was developed in Jena took its inspiration from Herder and Romanticism and it understands a people or a nation as humans connected by a spirit. This spirit may be something as mundane as sharing a language, moral values, rituals, habits, and a history, or it may be understood as a supernatural "essence" running through the people. Being a people is thus different from just being a collective of citizens of a state; peoplehood has a connective cultural or "spiritual" glue. Nationalism that has emerged from a Romantic connection through shared heritage and folklore is often referred to as Romantic Nationalism.

It is generally hard to figure out whether Romanticism, Idealism, and Romantic Nationalism as explored back then are in fact religious concepts that involve a metaphysical consciousness beyond human consciousness, or it is just a philosophical exploration of how a sense of peoplehood evolves and how we feel when we are awestruck by nature. These concepts were from the beginning, intimately intertwined with the thoughts on bildung towards higher stages of freedom, either as a civilization or regarding personal emancipation, which is not so much political freedom as it is the mastery of one's own feelings, servility, ambitions, idiosyncrasies, etc. Yet, the longing for political freedom runs as an undertone in the writings of all the young people engaging in these thoughts in and outside Jena, and beauty is a theme running through all of it as well.

Comparison:
developmental psychology vs. bildung

As shown above, there are some obvious similarities between modern developmental psychology and bildung, the way philosophers and poets defined bildung some 200 years ago. But there are also some differences.

The concept of bildung is intimately connected to the surrounding culture, to education, and to how we are embedded in its aesthetics and 'spirit'—and the 'spirit' in us. Bildung means becoming integrated in a symbolic world and emancipating oneself so that one can freely choose how one behaves and how one applies those symbols, i.e., uses the shared language and expresses oneself, and how one contributes to the culture. You have the symbols; they don't have you. Bildung is knowing your roots and having both an emotional connection to them and the ability to distance yourself from them; it is a richness of the cultural fabric in your mode of thinking and expression. Bildung is both a process and the result of that process. Bildung is a struggle with aesthetics, society, and culture, and bildung is intimately connected to pedagogy and andragogy ("adult pedagogy"), i.e., teaching, not least thanks to Rousseau and Pestalozzi.

The bildung philosophers were just that: philosophers. They did not have access to the academic knowledge about the human psyche that we have today. They did not have a scientific approach to our meaning-making, behavior, emotions, cognitive abilities, sense of self, the ego, etc. nor to how these develop as we mature. They had what modern scientists would call anecdotal evidence, and then they did some excellent thinking based on that.

Developmental psychology is an academic field that has emerged through the academic and systematic study of humans, our behavior, and the interpretation of our behavior. It is a field within the science of psychology, and it has refined its analyses through peer-reviewed inquiries.

Developmental psychology is an analytical tool and an empty structure. It can describe emotional, moral, and intellectual development and the development of one's sense of Self, the ego, but apart from individual therapy or coaching by a psychologist, developmental psychology itself does not offer personal development. One school of developmental psychology, Spiral Dynamics, concerns itself with cultural and societal, historical and political development, but Spiral Dynamics is also just an analytical tool; it does not provide culture or equip Spiral Dynamics practitioners to use culture for personal development. It offers no aesthetics, pedagogy or andragogy.

Generally, psychology is not interested in aesthetics, beauty, art, religion, rituals, lore, literature, and poetry, the shared symbolic world, which stirs our emotions; the cultural fabric that connects us spiritually, that speaks beyond what verbal language can express and that allows us to be meaning making with others. One major exception was psychologist Erich Fromm (1900-1980), who was both German, Jewish, and a philosopher. In his 1941 classic *Escape from Freedom,* he focused on our need for shared symbols, a shared symbolic world, in order for us to not despair. He coined the term "moral aloneness:" surrounded by people, one can be utterly alone if we do not share values, meaning-making and symbols, but one can also be stuck on a desert island and not feel alone if those values, meaning-making and symbols are intact and one knows that others are still using them (particularly if they are using them to not forget me while I am stuck on the island). The certainty that our inner worlds, to some extent, overlap makes life meaningful.

To use an image from architecture: Developmental psychology can tell whether you are a one, two, three, four, or five story building, and if you are a shiny castle or a run-down apartment building. It can also tell whether the rooms are furnished and how the stories are connected. What developmental psychology cannot do, but what bildung can do, on top of this is furnishing and decorating or pushing you to add another room, perhaps even another floor. Bildung can also allow you to choose the architectural style, the paint on the walls, the furniture, colors, if there should be antiques around, and art and souvenirs from journeys. Bildung allows you to decorate all rooms with a sense of personality and taste. If needed, bildung can go to the basement and pick heirlooms and acquisitions that are not generally in use, but which are suddenly needed.

With bildung, you can also understand this image and understand that it says nothing about the actual living and financial circumstances of the person in question, it is just an illustration of the complexity of a mind, not where somebody actually lives. Furthermore, the ability to come up with an image like that requires more than the emotional development that developmental psychology can describe, it requires a familiarity with, in this case, architecture, history, interior decoration AND bildung philosophy and developmental psychology so that they can be combined in an image and produce (hopefully) new meaning in the minds of others. (I considered for a while whether I should write that last sentence or not (I do have some measure of humility), and I reached the conclusion that it allowed me to make an important point: only because wise adults invested in my education did I acquire the frames of reference to create that image. My freedom to express myself increased.)

What bildung philosophy and developmental psychology share is the exploration of the development of our inner world; the complexity of our mind, our emotions, our consciousness, and our moral reasoning. As we mature, we transcend one way of being and develop another; a more complex way of being from which we can look back at our previous self, and then we can see that way of being from the outside. As teenagers, we can look back at our 10-year-old self and see how limited our understanding of the world and of our self was; at 35, we can look back at our teenage self and so forth. But we cannot, from the perspective of the younger self, look out at the older self, which is not there yet, and grasp it.

What bildung philosophy and developmental psychology also share is the understanding that the way we grow is through pushbacks: through having our worldview challenged, through meeting new challenges and through having to revise our assumptions. Through occasionally repainting and refurnishing a room, so to speak. Sometimes it may be even bigger than that: the plumbing leaks and you have to rip out and replace all the pipes in one wing of the building. According to both bildung philosophy and developmental psychology, we also grow through stepping up to new expectations and demands (somebody tells you it is time to add a sunroof and it must be Art Nouveau).

The bildung journey

What the bildung philosophers were very quick to understand, particularly Goethe, was that one thing that causes personal bildung to evolve and expand is travelling and living in another culture (country), i.e. to embark on a *bildungsreise*, a bildung journey. By having to live in another culture, by adjusting to it for some time, your perspective on the world changes. Not necessarily notably while you are still travelling, but you certainly discover it when you return home and are suddenly able to see your own culture through a new lens. Your epistemology has changed: you now have two epistemologies, and like having two eyes rather than just one, you have now gained perspective on both cultures and can see a new kind of depth in both of them.

If you cannot travel, you can explore the language, literature, and art from one or more other cultures at home, and the bildung philosophers of the 1790s understood this. They connected emotional, moral and cognitive development directly to enculturation, poetry, literature, the arts, beauty, aesthetics, education, and religion as well as to the beauty and vitality of nature. First, at home, then somewhere else, and then back home.

To have bildung means having culture, to have had that culture challenged, to encounter more than one culture, more than one epistemology, to have a major cultural pushback, and transcend one's first culture, to be aware of it, and to be able to both contain and transcend yourself and your culture through your own culture and then some.

Developmental psychology does not explore this.

Layers of bildung and ego-development

Seeing the development as consecutive phases has a lot of merit to it, but it also carries the risk of being too simplistic. It makes the understanding of our development too one-dimensional. Instead, we can see our development as layers upon layers added to our character. The human mind, our individual character, has a core, around which we develop new layers as we encounter life. We develop in many directions: we have cultural and emotional roots that can be shallow or deep, we have aspirations and plans that can be limited or lofty, and we can add knowledge and experience in many fields; we can broaden our horizons in all kinds of directions. We can thus see personal character as concentric spheres of added mental and emotional complexity:

Higher aspirations

Broader horizons — Infancy — Wider perspectives

1. Self-discovering
2. Self-consolidating
3. Self-governing
4. Self-authoring
5. Self-transforming

Deeper / stronger roots

Source: The Nordic Secret

Figure 1: Development Spheres

By looking at our bildung and emotional development like this, there is a horizontal plane of knowledge and a vertical axis of emotional depth and moral aspirations aiming upwards. We can thus talk about a rounded character, about our core self, inner complexity, and depth of character. We can 'look in' at ourselves rather than just 'back' and with still more knowledge, life-experience, pushbacks behind and inside us, our inner world isn't just expanding, it is becoming more complex and more roomy.

We can also talk about a rounded 11-year-old who knows what an 11-year-old should know in his or her culture, and who has the appropriate moral and emotional development for his or her age. Likewise, we can talk about a rounded or lopsided 35-year-old or 55-year-old where only part of the person has developed. What it means to be rounded is different at different ages, and it is not just a question of emotional structure, but also of knowledge and embeddedness in culture.

Food for thought

Have you ever gone on a journey that made you change something in your life when you came home?

FOLK-BILDUNG AND THE NORDICS

The Danish Spring

200 years ago, Denmark and the other Nordic countries were among the poorest in Europe. But as industrialization was about to wreak havoc to societal structures, a wise crown prince created public schools, and a generation later, a pastor and a school teacher figured out how to popularize bildung and create folk-bildung. A border conflict with Prussia then changed Denmark and the rest of the Nordics profoundly.

Shaftesbury was a British aristocrat, and Hume was technically of the nobility as well, though his family had lost their wealth. Rousseau, the German bildung philosophers, and Pestalozzi were all of the third estate with the rights and privileges of burghers. This was better than being a peasant or a serf, of course, but it was still a frustrating and often dangerous situation; kings and dukes could imprison and/or torture people without a trial for minor offenses, including insulting the ruler.

Among these philosophers, Pestalozzi was the only one who explicitly addressed the needs of the poor, be it peasants or city dwellers. The other philosophers either do not seem to have noticed the rest of the third estate at all, or seem to have more or less regarded the peasants as a natural resource or a picturesque, Romantic part of the landscape, and the city poor as an inevitable circumstance.

Not so in the Nordics.

Folk-bildung in Denmark

Around 1800, Denmark ruled over Norway, while Sweden ruled over Finland, and all four countries were among the poorest in Europe. Historical GDP per capita shows that the Nordics were on par with southern Europe and Russia; they were nowhere near the rich, industrialized Britain, Germany, France, Belgium, or Netherlands—or Switzerland, which had higher GDP per capita than any of them.[2] The Nordic poverty is interesting, because particularly Denmark, Norway, and Sweden had some of the highest literacy rates in Europe at the time; Sweden supposedly 100%. Literacy alone did not make an economic difference, not even compared to southern European countries that had not industrialized either.

In the 1780s, the Danish Crown Prince Regent Frederik (later Frederik VI), his cabinet and some other wise aristocrats realized that the old feudal system was challenged by industrialization, that Denmark needed land reforms, and that the peasants of the third estate needed much better education if they were to handle the changes and the reform. These people at the very top of Danish society were by no means thinking of giving up the feudal system, they were rather conservative, but they realized that an ignorant population would be to nobody's advantage. They started experimenting with better education at their personal estates, and in 1789, the Crown Prince Regent put together a school commission whose task it was to design the Danish school system of the future.

Among the members of the commission was Count Ernst Heinrich Schimmelmann (1747-1831) who had inherited his father's plantation in St. Croix. Ernst kept making fortunes on this plantation, his slaves and the sugar trade, the Schimmelmann family was the richest in Denmark, and he was the minister of finance. It was also Ernst and his circle of friends who corresponded with Schiller in 1793-94, and whose correspondence, after a rewrite became *Über die ästhetische Erziehung des Menschen, in einer Reihe von Briefen / On the Aesthetic Education of Man, a series of letters.*

Then came the Napoleonic Wars and, in short, the following happened: the British firebombed Copenhagen and stole the Danish navy

---

2   Bairoch 1976 and The Maddison Project 2014

in 1807, Denmark sided with Napoleon, Crown Prince Regent Frederik became King Frederik VI in 1808, Sweden lost Finland to Russia in 1809, Denmark went into a war with Sweden in 1813 and went bankrupt that same year due to the wars, and in 1814, Sweden got Norway from Denmark as a compensation for Finland. In the process, Norway got a rather liberal constitution in 1814, but leaving Denmark meant that Norway did not get the same progressive school legislation that Denmark gave itself that same year.

The Danish school commission had been working from 1789 to 1814 when they produced what has been called the most progressive school legislation of its time. It included seven years of mandatory education for all children, access to free public schools for all children, winter school available for all adults in the countryside for two hours per week, real schoolhouses, and appropriate education and training for the teachers. Due to the bankruptcy in 1813, however, Denmark could not afford all the good intentions right away. It was not until around 1840 that there were proper schoolhouses and trained teachers across the country and that the legislation had been fully implemented, but the course was set.

Nikolaj Frederik Severin Grundtvig

In 1802, Henrik Steffens, a young Norwegian Dane who had been studying in Jena with the German Romantic, Idealist philosophers, gave a series of lectures in Copenhagen about the spirit in peoples and in nature. To the audience, who were men of the Copenhagen bourgeoisie enlightened by the Enlightenment and thus spiritually starving, Steffens' Romantic words felt like rain on dry land. And yes, it was only the men; women were not allowed at public events like that.

In the audience was Steffens' 19-year-old cousin, Nikolaj Frederik Severin Grundtvig (1783-1872), a theology student and an ardent Protestant Christian. He did not think much of Steffens' and the German Idealists' "spirit," but he could not let go of the idea either. Rather than buying into it, he studied the German Idealists and bildung philosophers; he also studied Pestalozzi and whatever literature of lore he could get his hands on, including the Icelandic sagas, Greek mythology, Boewulf, and other grand narratives. Eventually, he reached the conclusion that the spirit could only be the Holy Spirit, and that the Holy Spirit would have different languages, traditions, songs, hymns, and folklore among different peoples in different places; the Danes had their Danish part of the Holy Spirit, the English had theirs and so forth. Grundtvig thus managed to unite the German Idealism with Christian theology.

From around 1810, when Grundtvig was in his 20s, he started translating the old Norse mythology into Danish, re-narrating some of it to fit his newly invented concept of the spirit. He also started writing song and hymn lyrics. Eventually, he became one of the most productive Danish lyricist with some 1,500 songs and hymns coming from his pen.

He also became a controversial pastor and public voice on Christianity, faith, culture, bildung, and politics, and in 1826, he was put under lifelong censure. By then, Grundtvig was 43 years old and though the censorship was very hard on him, it did not stop him from writing and translating; he was as productive as ever and got a grant to go to England to study some original Anglo-Saxon manuscripts.

Between 1829 and 1831, Grundtvig visited the UK three times, and the trips became transformative bildung journeys for him in a number of ways. He encountered English liberties, including liberty of religion, liberty of the press, and liberty of trade and commerce, and he discovered English pragmatism and parliamentarianism. He stayed at Cambridge University, and here he experienced the collegial relationship between professors and students, and how their discussions were fruitful explorations. All of it surprised, baffled and inspired him. Grundtvig also fell in love with a married woman, Clara Bolton, who stunned him with her intelligence and beauty.

The sum total of Grundtvig's trips to England was that he realized that women could be smart and engaged in the same issues as men, that disagreement and discussion are crucial parts of adult learning, and that the peasants may be capable of participating in the assemblies of the estates if they are educated and have bildung. In effect, but without expressing it that way, Grundtvig combined English pragmatism with German Idealism and Romanticism, and then he had an insight—and an idea began to dawn upon him.

The insight was that we need cultural identity and cultural diversity. We need to feel a sense of belonging and to know who we are. We need a people and a history; that's the identity. We also need to be able to express ourselves and to disagree in a civilized manner; that's the diversity. Peoplehood is not uniformity, quite the contrary, it is the ability to disagree and look at things differently, while sharing the spirit that allows us to feel attached to one another and to care about our country together. Grundvig expressed this in a famous line in a poem in 1832: *Freedom for Loke as well as for Thor;* not just the obviously noble Thor must enjoy freedom, the trickster, Loke, who brings out chaos, must have freedom too.

The idea that began to take shape in Grundtvig's mind was that in order to create this shared identity and diversity, a new kind of school was necessary. The first time Grundtvig explored this was in 1836 when he wrote his first pamphlet about a 'school for life.' In this first exploration of the new kind of school, it just concerned the education for young men who were to become, for instance, civil servants. As things were, the young men studied too much Greek and Latin; dry book-knowledge, dead letters, not spirited, living words, not Danish. Rather than bookworms who mastered the classics, the Danes deserved civil servants who knew their own people, its culture, and its (Holy) spirit.

Few Danes understood what Grundvig was trying to say, and by 1838, he was so disappointed he wrote another pamphlet suggesting that the Danes were too dumb to understand the idea about a 'school for life,' but the Norwegians would no doubt be smarter! Grundtvig's faith in the Norwegians may have been influenced by the fact that he had many fans in Norway and that they had crowdfunded financial support for him while he was under censorship (it was lifted 1837). With the pamphlet suggesting that the Norwegians were smarter than the Danes, Grundtvig became even more popular in Norway.

That same year, Grundtvig tried to clarify his thinking for the Danes once more, but he had also reached a new insight: this school for life should not just be for the bourgeoisie boys who got a high-school or college degree; this should be a folk-high-school for the people themselves! The people, i.e., the farmers and peasants, should have access to education beyond the seven years of primary school, and this education should promote their sense of Danishness so that they could care about their country! The content should be Danish history, world history, Bible studies, literature, particularly the Icelandic Sagas, discussions, and basic knowledge about their country, how it was run, what was produced, and what the economy looked like. Since this was a school for life, not a school for a diploma, there should be no tests and no exams. Life itself should be the exam: Will this young person go out into life, find purpose and meaning, serve God and country, and make a difference? Since Grundtvig was a brilliant lyricist and preacher but a horrible writer of prose, still nobody understood what he was trying to say.

Nevertheless, the basic idea that farmers and peasants needed to understand that they were Danish and that they belonged to a nation caught on.

Denmark and Schleswig-Holstein

The need for Danish self-awareness among the rural population was not least because Denmark was in a precarious situation regarding the border with the German Confederation and Prussia. Between Denmark proper and German Mecklenburg and Prussia were the two duchies Schleswig and Holstein, which were (and still are) hyphenated Schleswig-Holstein because culturally and economically, they worked as a unit. At the time, they were also the most industrialized and richest area under the Danish king. Their legal status, though, was not that they were part of Denmark, but that they were the personal property of the King of Denmark. The people in Schleswig-Holstein were culturally a mix of Danes and Germans, and given some Schleswig-Holsteiners' desire for an independent constitution and closer ties with the German states plus a Prussian desire for Schleswig-Holstein, some influential Danes began to consider the establishment of a Danish folk-high-school in Schleswig. If the young farmers in Schleswig-Holstein could *feel* Danish, there would be less of a risk they would be lured towards the much richer German states and Prussia, and in case of an invasion, they would defend Denmark and their Danishness.

Some pastors and wealthy farmers of the Danish persuasion therefore began to look for funding and started selling shares in order to establish the first folk-high-school, and in 1844, they opened *Rødding Højskole* / Rødding Folk-high-school in the village Rødding in the northern, most Danish part of Schleswig. The schoolhouse was a handsome three-story building with, for the time, impressive separate wings: a barn, stables, dormitory, and, as farmhouses go, a generous house that served as the home of the headmaster, Dr. Phil and pastor Christian Flor (1792-1875). The young farmers should not only learn who they were and to what country and spirit they belonged, they should also learn the latest and most advanced agricultural techniques and useful science. The initiators, the investors, Grundtvig, Grundtvig's fans, and Danes of a strong sense of Danishness in general, had very high hopes for the school. It turned out to be a modest success, though. It had a two-year program, it was too expensive for anybody but the wealthiest farmers' sons, and there was something missing.

The fateful year: 1848

King Frederik VI, who created the school legislation in 1814, had died in 1839, and his cousin, Christian Frederik, became his successor, King Christian VIII. With a new king, the Danish bourgeoisie had been very much looking forward to getting a constitution resembling the Norwegian constitution, but no such thing happened; Christian VIII was perfectly happy with absolute monarchy. In January 1848, Christian VIII died and was succeeded by Frederik VII, and, again, the bourgeoisie hoped that absolute monarchy would finally be over, and Denmark could get a constitution. Again that did not happen, though some legislation was liberalized, e.g., regarding freedom of expression.

In February 1848, revolutions broke out across Europe, and the Schleswig-Holstein movement for an independent Schleswig-Holstein joined the liberal German movement.

This fueled the political debate in Denmark regarding a constitution, and in March, Denmark proper almost had a revolution too. In Copenhagen, on March 21st, people marched to the royal castle to demand a liberal constitution from the new king Frederik VII: they wanted a tripartition of the political power. They also wanted the king to give up the more German Holstein duchy so that a constitution could include the more Danish Schleswig duchy, i.e., a separation of Schleswig and Holstein. The protestors also wanted a new government with liberal ministers rather than the conservative ones they already had.

King Frederik VII was not willing to give up his duchy, but he was OK with the Danes getting a liberal constitution, a parliament, and some suffrage as long as he could remain king. Since the hope had never been to overthrow the monarchy, the Copenhagen protesters accepted: absolute monarchy was to be abolished, and a constitutional board was put together. Interestingly enough, both Grundtvig (who was an ardent anti-democrat) and Christian Flor from Rødding Højskole became members of the board.

This turn of events did not please the Schleswig-Hosteiners who wanted to remain united, and on March 24th 1848, the First Schleswig War broke out. It was initially a civil war in Schleswig, but soon it became a war between Denmark and Prussia over the two duchies, which meant that Danish nationalism went through the roof!

Having been promised a constitution, the Danes rallied around their king and would not allow Schleswig to be lost to Prussia. They believed in the war, got new uniforms, composed patriotic songs, sent their young men towards the duchies, and entered Denmark into three years of war.

On June 5th 1849, i.e., during the war, Denmark got its first liberal constitution. By modern standards, it was not impressive, as only some 10-15% of men could vote, and until 1901, the ballots were not secret, and women did not get suffrage until 1915. But it made the Danes happy.

In 1851, the war over the status of Schleswig and Holstein came to an armistice. At the peace negotiations in London in 1851-52, it was agreed among Denmark, Prussia and Austria that Schleswig and Holstein would each have their own constitution like Denmark, that there was to be a joint constitution for Schleswig, Holstein and Denmark, and that Schleswig could not have a stronger connection to Denmark than Holstein. About this, the Danes were not happy: they wanted Schleswig to be Danish.

Collective nation bildung

It may seem like a strange thing to map out a border conflict like that in a book about bildung, but this border conflict and the constitution had a crucial influence on bildung in Denmark: at the collective level, in the individual minds and institutionally.

In the spring of 1848, at the collective level, the nation suddenly became very visible to all. There was the promise of the constitution that was new and exciting, and then the war broke out, and across Denmark, the spirit changed: the 'We, the Danes' became visible. Not least because all those young men trained and marched to the battlefield in their uniforms; previous wars had typically been king against king with mercenary armies, now the sons of the nation were called upon to fight for their country for honor and glory.

In the individual minds, something changed too.

In 1848, 18-year-old Mathilde Fibiger (1830-1872) was the house teacher of two children of a wealthy farmer who lived on a small island some 100 kilometers south of Copenhagen where she grew up. The provincial, petit-bourgeois environment drove her nuts. So, she wrote a novel about it: *Clara Raphael: Tolv Breve / Clara Raphael: Twelve Letters*. It was a letter novel, very autobiographical, hilariously funny, and NOT to the taste of the sleepwalking bourgeoisie, including her father. The book caused a scandal, her father was furious, and he even traveled all the way to the island and took her home.

Apart from mocking the bourgeoisie for being a grey mass of greyness from which it was impossible to discern the contours of anything, Fibiger was excited about Denmark, the political development, and the war. From the novel:

> The 21st of March, a new life dawned for me. I saw the Danish people, whom I had only known from sagas and songs; I heard the words spoken, which found the deepest resonance in my soul. My ideals greeted me in real life and my heart beat with proud self-consciousness. When I saw the Danish national colors, read about the war, or met a brave countryman soldier who was about to leave, then something stirred me in the depth of my chest, like when in a strange country one hears the beloved melody of one's mother tongue. And along with my fatherland I received faith in God! It was as if the sun came out and woke me up from a long dream. I felt what it was like to be a human being, created in God's image, created for an eternal life.

This is a socialized self reflecting with surprise on the developmental change that had taken place; a sudden transformation from self-consolidating ego-layer 2, lukewarm 2½ or coerced self-governing ego-layer 3 to a passionate ego-layer 3: self-governing with enthusiasm! With that intense connection to fellow countrymen, one can suddenly put duty above self, and one can see the purpose of living up to others' expectations. In fact, one would probably strive to exceed such expectations.

Later, Fibiger describes a friend and this shows perfectly well the difference in perspective between ego-layer 2, self-consolidating, and 3, self-governing:

> She is passionate about little things, I about grand ones. I love all the soldiers as brothers because they fight for our common cause; she only cares about the cause because she knows a couple of the officers.

An inner transformation like this took place among Danes of all so-cial backgrounds, and this new shared sense of Danishness contributed to breaking down at least some of the old conceptions of the different strata in society, the estates. Whether one was a sharecropper, a worker, or of the bourgeoisie or aristocracy, everybody was suddenly Danish, not just legally but in spirit. There was still plenty of old feudal thinking going around, and society was still extremely hierarchical, but at least the share-croppers were Danish sharecroppers, and the bourgeoisie, aristocracy, and bureaucrats were Danish bourgeoisie, aristocracy and bureaucrats.

What is truly remarkable about young Fibiger is that she so obviously wrote her novel from a self-authoring, layer 4 perspective at age 18. She also lived to become both a controversial cultural figure, a sort of sad fate, loathed and dismissed, and the first female telegraphist and civil servant in Denmark.

Christen Kold

One of the Danish men who almost desperately wanted to fight for Den-mark in the war in 1848 was Christen Kold (1816-1870). Unfortunately (or maybe not), he was too clumsy to load a rifle, and the army dismissed him. This threw him into an identity crisis, and he considered emigrat-ing to the US, but instead, he ended up going with a Danish missionary pastor and his family to Smyrna in Turkey as the house teacher of the pastor's children.

Kold was trained and worked as a teacher from when he was 20, but he never fitted into the school system. He found the Danish schoolbook at the time useless. He also found the rote learning and memorizing of everything from hymnbook verses to names and years of Danish kings meaningless—as did the children. What he discovered, though, was that when he told stories, the children listened and lit up.

In Smyrna, Kold taught the pastor's children and also found time to become a bookbinder and saved up some money binding books. He also got terribly homesick, and in 1850, he could not stand it anymore, he bought a boat ticket to Trieste, in Trieste, he bought a handcart for his belongings and then he walked all the way up through Europe to his hometown, Thisted, in the northern part of Jutland, Denmark.

He undoubtedly did some serious soul searching during all that walking and considered what to do next. Similar to the success he had had telling stories to school children, he had found that adults listened and lit up when he read aloud great stories. Not only did they listen, it was as if something happened to them at a spiritual level. Kold was particularly successful at this when he read some of the novels by the Danish Romantic poet Bernhard Severin Ingemann (1789-1862); these were great heroic stories about Denmark's medieval past.

Over the years, Kold had read many of the German bildung philosophers and everything by Pestalozzi he could get his hands on, he also read Grundtvig, and he realized that school had to be about more than just dissemination of knowledge. People had to be touched; they had to be awakened. A teacher also had to share some of his own story and invest his soul in it. There had to be a relationship; teaching was not a one-way endeavor; it had to go both ways.

There also needed to be a purpose with the bildung and the education promoting it. What Kold wanted to create was a 'homesickness' after Danishness and good citizenship. Education should not just be for better skills and more knowledge, it should be the moral and aesthetic development Schiller had written about, and it should awaken the spirit. What Kold wanted to create (or re-create) was "the spirit of 1848;" the spirit that young Fibiger had also explored in her novel.

In 1851, Kold started the first school for just that: Ryslinge Folk-high-school in the village Ryslinge on the island Funen. Through his own savings, support from Grundtvig and people around Grundtvig, Kold found enough money to buy a farmhouse, he moved in, and 15 young men aged 18 to mid-20s joined him.

Kold did not write much, but there is a transcript of him telling his story at a meeting in Copenhagen organized by Grundtvig in September 1866. The text conveys very well what spirit the schools were started in, and how our sense of peoplehood and national identity today was new and strange to people 150-200 years ago. Here Kold in 1866, speaking about 1851:

There were already a lot of awakened people, and at that time they also became Danish. The songs from "The Danish Society" were sung throughout the country, but of course not by all people. There was a lot of life and enthusiasm from 1848, which left some traces, and then it really struck me how the spirit works in general. Earlier, I had only known how the spirit worked through the word, partly on myself and partly from me to my neighbor, in the individual; but at that time, I knew that all people had been endowed with spirit, and it was then that I first became acquainted with the Danish spirit. That was also when I got a clearer idea of what I really wanted to produce, namely, that feeling and enthusiasm of 1848; the revival that took place then should stay and be confirmed. Through school and by the word, I wanted to make sure that all Danish people could be lastingly excited. (...)

I would need a house that could accommodate at least 14-15 people, and then I hoped that awakened folks would be so good to send me their children to try it out, so that we could get started and tell people what we really wanted to accomplish, namely to awaken both the Christian spirit and the Danish spirit, and make people believe in God's love and Denmark's happiness. (...)

A number of so-called Grundtvigians had gathered in Copenhagen to figure out what could be done to enlighten the Danish peasantry so that they could use the civil freedom that they had been given, and the spirit must have pulled a few strings, because when it was agreed that something should be done and they asked who should carry out this task, Louis Kristian Müller replied: I know none but Kold, and they all found that this was the right man. (...)

On November 1st, 15 students came driving with their finest horses and carts and they looked so happy. They were happy because they had made it and gotten away from home. And I was so happy I've never known such joy in my life, though I have been very, very happy. Then we started with Ingemann's novels, because we had to start where they were; what we had already learned, we knew, and what we did not know, we could not begin with. From Grundtvig's World History I read a few pieces here and there and sought to point out a little of the connection between ancient times, the Middle Ages and the present, but the students did not seem able to comprehend it, but they understood Ingemann's historical novels. Nevertheless, the goal was reached, and none of them have lost the spirit they received at the time. It is clearly visible, whether they vote for the parliament or something must be done in order to make Denmark great as it used to be; they have often strengthened those who were hard pressed in such struggles.

One thing that was radically different at Kold's school in Ryslinge compared to the one in Rødding was that, like Pestalozzi, Kold lived not just at the school like Christian Flor, but along with the students; he created a homey feeling and took upon himself the role of householder at the school. Not only was everybody there on equal terms, though he was their teacher, it was the same relaxed atmosphere the young people knew from their own homes. Kold had also realized that his program should be no longer than five months, and it should be affordable; if somebody could only afford three months, that was fine too.

The other fateful year: 1864

Kold's school was a success with the youngsters who went there, and one or two new folk-high-schools opened each year the following years. The idea caught on, but slowly.

That changed in 1864. That year, Denmark got itself into a new war over Schleswig-Holstein, this time with Bismarck on the other side, and Prussia ended up taking both duchies. This meant that half the peninsula of Jutland or 1/3 of the Danish landmass was suddenly lost. The defeat sent a shock wave through Denmark, the Danes, and the Danish spirit: First Denmark lost Norway to Sweden, then Schleswig did not become entirely Danish, and now this! And all those good Danes who were now under Prussian rule, how could they remain Danish? And what would become of Denmark, if Bismarck decided to take the rest of the country as well?

The Danes figured it out: folk-high-schools! Strengthen the Danish spirit, study history, study science, sing nationalistic songs, study Icelandic Sagas and the Bible, improve reading and writing skills, learn how to use the latest technology, study political science and economy, but first and foremost: ask questions, explore together and learn to think for yourself, ignite the spirit, liberate the mind!

The defeat in 1864 sparked a folk-high-school movement, and in 1865, five new schools opened across Denmark, in 1866, four new schools, in 1867, 17 schools, and in 1868, 11 schools. By 1900, a total of 135 folk-high-schools had been established in Denmark, and some 110 of them had survived and were still taking in a new batch of students twice a year. Each school had between 20 and 70 students, the average probably around 30-40.

110 schools in a country of roughly 3.8 million people in the years around 1900, may not sound like a lot, but this was not a government program, these were schools started by local pastors, farmers, and philanthropists over the course of one generation. The Danish government was not slow to see the potential, though, and started subsidizing the schools at least as early as 1867, but the government stayed completely out of the programs and the content. In fact, the schools were very adamant about their freedom.

If one does the math, the number of students is interesting, not least because this development did not take place in the bourgeoisie but among farmers, peasants and sharecroppers. It was not the very poorest but the middle and upper-middle parts of the rural population who now got access to the latest knowledge and to asking questions—on top of seven years of primary school.

Given the typical number of students at each school in 1867, the total number of folk-high-school students in Denmark must have been around 1,000, perhaps twice as many (say, 35 students in 30 schools, two times per year ≈ 2,000). In 1870 it must have been 2,000-4,000 students, in the late 1890s 4,500+, and from 1900-1940 there must have been on average at least 6,000 Danes per year who went to a folk high school, half of them women. With an annual cohort of 63,000 in the late 1800s, that would have been close to 10%. By 1940, that meant, give or take some deaths and migration, some 200,000 out of 2.5 million adults in Denmark had been at a folk high school in their youth; among adult farmers and peasants alone, that may have meant at least 15%.

Imagine what it would do to a country, if around 10% of the annual cohort got a sparkle in their eyes, developed an appreciation for studying, dared ask questions and thought for themselves, felt a desire to become local community organizers, took over a farm, started applying the latest technology and science, partook in starting cooperative grocery stores, dairies, bacon factories, and slaughterhouses, and took responsibility for their country.

That's what happened.

Transforming a nation

Other things happened in Denmark from around 1850, of course. Denmark got railways, all areas of education improved, particularly the education of engineers and veterinarians, who helped improve Danish meat and dairy production considerably.

But one should not overlook the implications of the way Denmark was educated and energized from the bottom and up. In Norway and Sweden, pastors, farmers, intellectuals, and even some industrialists were quick to notice, and both countries had their first folk-high-schools in the 1860s. Finland started their first folk-high-schools in the 1870s.

Since the reason for starting folk-highs-schools in Denmark was so obvious: 'We cannot afford to lose our Danish spirit if Prussia takes our country!' there was never any doubt why Denmark needed folk-high-schools. The sell was harder in Norway and Sweden.

In Norway, the local farmers and sharecroppers were hesitant to send their sons and daughters to a folk-high-school. Particularly because the students did not get a diploma, they just learned useful things and developed their character. Eventually, Norwegian parents and youth began to see the value in that as well.

In Sweden, suffrage was expanded to all property owning men in 1866, which meant that farmers who had no training in understanding legislation, hosting meetings, doing bookkeeping, working democratically etc. suddenly got political influence, could start local party chapters, could run for parliament etc. Much of the reason for the Swedish bourgeoisie and others in power to support folk-high-schools in Sweden was thus the realization that this new class of voters needed to understand their political power, the limits to their political power, and 'What is Sweden?' These new skills along with new agricultural skills and science, were the key to the success of the Swedish folk-high-schools, the spiritual and nationalistic aspects less so.

In Finland, the first folk-high-school opened in 1874, but the country was under Russian rule until 1918, and a nationalistic agenda was tricky and could not be explicit. There is no doubt, though, that the cultural self-awareness played a crucial role in the Finnish folk-high-schools.

How deep an impact the schools had on Danish youth and their society is described in a Norwegian book about Christen Kold from 1911, *Ein Folkelarar / A Folk Teacher* by the Norwegian teacher Andreas Austlid (1851-1926). When Austlid was 28 years old and had been a teacher for eight years, he visited some Danish folk high schools in 1879-81, and he was both intimidated and inspired by the young Danes he met there:

It was a rich life in which I found myself. To me, the kid from Gudbrand, it was mostly too strong. They both enchanted and intimidated me. I had never met such open and trusting young people. (...)

They were so happy and friendly that it came crackling off them. Clever and good-spirited constantly. But when they talked about their future and all the things they wanted to do, then I was scared. (...)

O, so playfully light they perceived their future, these youngsters! They were almost childlike. Everybody was going to do something; everybody was going to be something. And these were not small things either. But believe they did so that the sparks were flying. Doubt probably did not exist in their dictionary—and speak they did, more than was good, I found. Had this been up in Norway, people would just have laughed at them: "Children. Smart alecks, not dry behind their ears yet," that is what the Gudbrands people would have said about them.

But here, those daydreamers went around in bright daylight and built castles in the air.

A guy from Funen wanted to return to his father's farm and shake things up, create a new state-of-the-art farm—and change the entire parish. The neighbors should rub the sleep out of their eyes and copy him!

Another just had a bit of sharecropper's land and two cows. But he would compete with the farmer, develop horticulture, have 20 pigs and 200 chickens, get more than two cows, and sell more from his small lot than the big farms. (...)

Something had happened here, I had to say. Where did they get this strong, light belief?

From the free school teachers, the folk high school teachers, some pastors, and some farmers here and there—who had tried to live according to this and found that it was true, they said.

But where had they gotten it from? I dug into the matter and asked.

From Grundtvig and from Kold. Yes, it was always the same answer.

To what extent Norwegian, Swedish and Finnish youth became as excited as the Danes is hard to tell, since it was the Danish case that was used as the selling point in the other three countries. There is no doubt, though, that as young people across the Nordics applied their new bildung, they changed their countries.

Nordic folk-bildung

In the late 1880s, academics started folk-bildung for workers in Copenhagen, Oslo, and Stockholm, such as lectures, guided museum tours, and popular science publications that spread beyond the capitals. Around 1900, workers themselves organized folk-bildung in the major towns in Scandinavia.

In 1902, the Swedish teacher and Social Democrat, Oscar Olsson (1877-1950), invented the study circle. Study circles do not have a teacher, instead people self-organize with one person leading the circle, organizing the meetings, and finding the study material; everybody then commits to the circle itself and contributes with their thoughts and questions regarding the topic. In the early 1900s, this meant that even in remote villages people could self-organize folk-bildung in their homes, and typically, they just bought one copy of a book, everybody read it, then they discussed it, and afterwards, the book belonged to their shared library. The study circle has come to characterize the folk-bildung in Sweden, and the former Swedish prime minister, Olof Palme (1927-1986) called Sweden a "study circle democracy."

Beginning in the 1920s, study associations of all political persuasions proliferated throughout the Nordic countries. The content was a mix of language courses and learning new professional skills such as typing, but there were also classes on economic theory, art, science, history, and much more.

Crucial in the Nordics were also the sports associations, which played a role in straightening up both city and rural youth and teaching people to do organizational work; i.e., besides the sports, it was democratic training. The Nordics also had a host of temperance societies and independent churches, and the scouts played a crucial role for children in the Nordics as they did around the globe.

A Danish specialty for the children

Denmark also has the so-called *efterskoler / after-schools*. The 'after' refers to being after confirmation and the schools are unique to Denmark. The first school was started in 1879 and they are very much like the folk-high-schools, but for the 14-18-yearolds. They offer 1-year programs, which include the standard curriculum for the last year of primary school and they give a diploma.

Three phases of Nordic folk-bildung

The folk-bildung of the folk-high-schools that focused on a national sense of peoplehood and the latest science and technology, plus the study circles, and the evening classes in the cities, we can call **folk-bildung 1.0**. This first wave of folk-bildung empowered the rural and working-class populations and allowed them to become active citizens and grab the new opportunities of the industrialized society. The outcome was enthusiastic self-governing young adults, who were ready to become self-authoring as adults once they got involved in their society, joined unions, voted, and maybe ran for a political party.

Folk-bildung 2.0 would be a cultural wave that is unique to the Nordic countries: Cultural Radicalism. The earliest Cultural Radical thinkers were Danish cultural critic Georg Brandes (1842-1927) and Norwegian playwright Henrik Ibsen (1828-1906) in the 1880s. In the 1930s, Cultural Radicalism caught momentum, not least due to Danish architect Poul Henningsen and his design as well as his lyrics.

Cultural Radicalism is an Enlightenment and emancipation ideology and idealism that wants to rid culture of old superstitions, religion, oppression, and conservative norms in general. It promoted enlightenment, science, nature, rationalism, universalism, human equality, human dignity, sexual liberation, and democracy. It was outspoken anti-communist, anti-fascist, anti-nazi, and anti-nationalistic, and it mocked the oppressive aspects of marriage, a critique that felt highly offensive to many in the 1930s.

The reason Cultural Radicalism can be called folk-bildung 2.0 is that it was not just an intellectual movement, it had a culture changing and enlightening agenda, which materialized through aesthetics: art, architecture, design, and some of the most powerful lyrics and satirical songs of the 1930s and 1940s. In many ways, Cultural Radicalism mirrored the German wave of modernism, futurism, Art Deco, and Bauhaus, but it had humans at the center, not technology, industry, speed, and "machine-ism." Cultural Radicalism challenged existing norms and dehumanization by showing an alternative through poetry, satire, and new design of everyday items. The design was practical, minimalistic, and based on ideas about the quality of life, a certain frugality, equality, and humanism. The backdrop was always emancipation, human proportions, nature, natural materials, and letting go of old norms and oppression. Cultural Radicalism did not have today's psychological vocabulary, but what the Cultural Radicals were aiming for was self-authoring: emancipation from old norms and finding your true self and individual path in life. Everything that the authoritarian and totalitarian mass-movements of the 1930s were not.

Cultural Radicalism came to define the Nordics in the aftermath of WWII, particularly in the educational system, in folk-high-schools and in folk-bildung in general. Beginning in the 1950s, and particularly since the 1970s, this also meant that the folk-high-schools have focused less on history and a shared sense of peoplehood, and have shifted their attention towards personal pursuits in the arts and sports, and on getting a European and global outlook. The schools have since been less outspoken and have not defined the cultural agenda philosophically or intellectually as they did in the 1800s. The major exceptions are a couple of schools that were established in the aftermath of WWII and had specific democratic and humanitarian agendas. Since the 1970s, as the general level of education went up, and as public libraries and national public radio and television reached all strata of the Nordic societies, the folk-high-schools have been more directed towards self-authoring in a globalized world than self-governing in a nation-state.

After 150 years of parallel development from common roots, the folk-bildung in Denmark, Norway, Sweden, and Finland still have much in common, but there are also major structural differences. Among the commonalities are that this is an educational sector beyond the formal education of primary, secondary, and tertiary education. The schools are not commercial but organized through either democratic associations, communities of faith, political parties, or unions, and though there is state or municipality financial support, they are not run by the state, and they have complete freedom regarding the content.

At the beginning of the 21st century, folk-high-schools across the Nordics are as popular as ever. Young people, in particular, needing a gap year flock at the folk-high-schools in order to find their calling before choosing tertiary education. Not only is the world becoming more complex and demanding, the focus on PISA and other tests in formal education is taking the meaning and joy out of learning. Whoever can afford it (which is not everybody), seeks (folk-)bildung and nourishment of their spirit and soul.

What is lacking throughout the Nordics is the folk-bildung idea that is as radical in our time as folk-bildung 1.0 and 2.0 were in theirs. We have not yet come up with the meaning-making bildung of the 21st century that will allow us to recalibrate ourselves and our societies to the local, national, continental, and global challenges we are facing. We need folk-bildung 3.0.

Food for thought

Are there people who should NOT enjoy bildung?

MORE AND BETTER BILDUNG

A deeper understanding

Bildung is always bildung in a context. Cultural codes define collective norms, not least regarding freedom and responsibility. Nationalism tends to have a bad reputation today, but if Danish folk-bildung was so nationalistic, why was that not a problem? Or was it? Nationalism is important to millions of people; are they wrong, or do they and their nationalism represent a potential source of global change for a sustainable future? What kind of bildung would that require? Can we develop enough education and bildung for everybody to lead meaningful lives in the 21st century? A *Bildung Rose* offers a deeper understanding, and so do Circles of Belonging. Lack of bildung manifests itself in many ways, and we need a toolbox to deal with it.

In order to understand the 'mechanics' of what happened in Denmark, this chapter offers a set of prisms through which to see bildung and folk-bildung. Hopefully, this will allow us to have a qualified conversation about bildung and folk-bildung, past, present, and future, so that we can develop more of it. Hopefully, we can also develop folk-bildung 3.0.

Cultural codes and societal transformation

Bildung is always bildung in a cultural and societal context, and bildung philosophy has been aware of this since 1774; the power structures of society as well as culture, poetry, aesthetics, literature etc. are essential to bildung.

Cultural codes are the structures and epistemologies of society that change and must change as societies grow in size and complexity. They define the distribution of freedom and responsibility throughout society, and they are thus the moral fabric that can keep violence at a minimum as more people need to live, collaborate, compete, and thrive in bigger societies within certain physical boundaries. Today's cultural theorists generally refer to four cultural codes: pre-historic indigenous, pre-modern, modern, and postmodern cultural code. All four cultural codes define much of what is necessary bildung in order to thrive in a particular society:

- **Pre-historic indigenous code:** emerged among hunter--gatherer tribes of, typically, 50-80 people (maximum 150ish), where oral narrative was the most advanced means of communication. These small societies were egalitarian, humans considered themselves a part of nature and its cycles, and both humans, human made tools and nature were imbued with spirits that related to one another, and that one had to treat with great respect.
- **Premodern code:** emerged in the city states of the Bronze Age (from around 3500 BCE in the Middle-East and Egypt) and the Iron Age (from around 1100 BCE along the climate belt from Greece across Asia to China and Japan). These were societies of 5,000-100,000 people connected in million strong empires. Writing text by hand was the most advanced communication technology, and these big societies needed hierarchies of power in order to hold together. Patriarchy and organized religion emerged, and humans were increasingly seen as being separate from nature.
- **Modern code:** emerged in Western societies of millions of people, first initiated and made possible by the invention of the printing press with movable type and later held together by mass media; newspapers at first, then electronic media

like radio and television. These (Western) societies developed science, equal rights for all and democracy. Humans are not only considered to be outside nature; through our technological development, we have convinced ourselves that we can control nature.

- **Postmodern code:** emerged in a globalized world where minorities are entitled to their existence and dignity, where people move around and keep their culture, and where social media with global reach ignores national borders and makes every culture a minority culture. With all this diversity, living, studying, and working next to one another, no one truth seemed to be able to prevail, irony took its place, and political correctness became shorthand for not offending anybody and not creating hostile environments. Under the postmodern code, humans are now so far away from nature that both sex and gender are believed to be social constructs; biological human females are not considered to be women, but vagina owners.

It is telling, perhaps, that when the bildung philosophers explored our moral and emotional development, they were living through a radical cultural change from premodern, religious, feudal, agricultural absolute monarchies to modern, enlightened democratic, industrialized nation states. The societal, cultural fabric was in upheaval, and the human ability to interact with society and others was explored as something equally dynamic.

Our own time is also a time of grand transition. Modernity has been challenged by postmodernism for a generation now, but neither modernity nor postmodernism on their own is sufficient as a shared cultural code. Modernity grew from and helps us navigate the industrialized nation state, but modernity is not complex enough to handle our inner spiritual needs, nor a globalized world facing global climate change and other changes to nature, a global economy, millions of people migrating, and billions of people connected by social media across borders. Postmodernism is good at deconstructing culture and society, but it is terrible at bringing people together; it is only good at taking things apart. Hence, the education and bildung of the two are insufficient too. Just like premodern education and bildung became insufficient 200 years ago.

To explore what bildung could mean in the 21st century, we need to consider what could come after postmodernism. One suggestion is metamodernity, which I have explored in *Metamodernity; Meaning and Hope in a Complex World* (Nordic Bildung, 2019).

- **Metamodern code**: integration and appreciation of the best from all of the four codes above into one connected whole. Metamodernity is nowhere yet, but it is emerging and can become a multilayered cultural code with a complexity that matches the complexity of the world that we have created and keep bringing forth.

One interesting feature of the first four codes is that the cultural code of the lesser complex society cannot grasp the cultural code of the more complex society. From the point of view of the lesser complex society, the more complex society looks amoral. Conversely, from the point of view of the more complex society, the lesser complex society with the older cultural code is usually interpreted as primitive. There is a conflict between codes. From the perspective of metamodernity, the previous codes are all perceived as containing something crucial to being human:

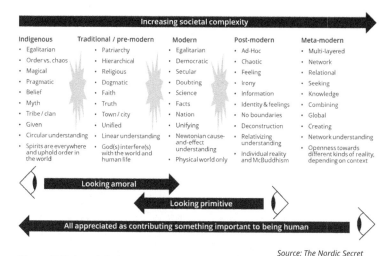

Figure 2: Cultural Codes

Source: The Nordic Secret

Within any one of the four cultural codes, one can have highly advanced knowledge and experience, and one can be self-consolidating, self-governing, self-authoring, or self-transforming, it just may not be equally appreciated.

The Wellbeing Matrix (next page) shows how, in pre-historic indigenous culture, life may have been easier when self-governing, but all ego-layers or phases of ego-development seem to have been appreciated: shamans and wise elders were held in high esteem. In pre-modern societies (historically and the ones that are still around), only self-governing was/is allowed, and people who cannot play by the rules suffer harsh punishments, people who are thinking for themselves and foolish enough to express it, likewise. If we take premodern Europe, the self-consolidating 'what's in it for me'-people were publicly shamed, the self-authoring 'I can think for myself'-people were burned by the stake. In modern societies, one may live long and happy as self-governing, but one only gets to live life to the fullest as self-authoring. Postmodernism makes nobody truly happy, but we have developed the psychopharmaceuticals to

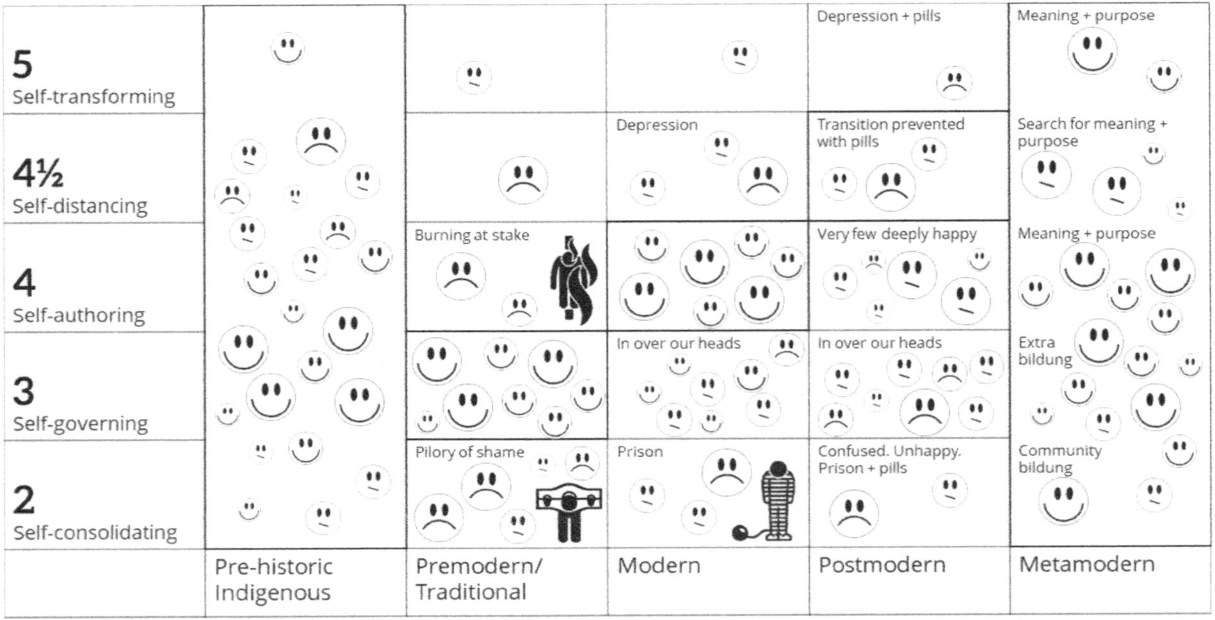

Source: The Nordic Secret

Figure 3: The Wellbeing Matrix

cover it up. Hopefully, metamodernity will appreciate all phases of life and the layers of personal development that match them.

We can be highly educated within indigenous, premodern, modern, or postmodern code and still not be able to navigate any of the three other codes. Bildung philosophy is aware of this: we are fundamentally shaped by the civilization within which we are raised, not just in the self-governing phase, but throughout life. Unless we transcend our own culture through a bildung journey: live in a foreign place, make a fool out of ourselves, feel ashamed, learn from it, and start navigating according to the foreign code.

The cultural codes show how both individual freedom and responsibility have increased over the course of history. One of the problems Western culture has suffered due to postmodernism is the lack of value hierarchies; a postmodern society cannot explain why modernity is better than pre-modernity. Metamodernity allows us to state that the increasing freedom and responsibility is an objective good, and it allows us to argue why some societies are better than others. It also shows why metamodernity will be better than any of the other codes, but we need to create the bildung and folk-bildung it requires. Bildung 3.0 would have to be metamodern and enrich us through elements of all four previous codes if society is to transition peacefully and meaningfully into metamodernity.

Freedom and responsibility

Freedom is key in bildung and so is responsibility. The bildung philosophers focused very much on the first, not explicitly so much on the latter; probably because they lived in a premodern feudal society with so many obligations and so little freedom, be it political freedom, economic freedom or freedom to choose your own path in life. What was left was the existential freedom: transcending your own emotions through the norms of society, then transcending the norms of society by allowing your own emotions and your own thinking to give you autonomy and a personal moral compass.

Nevertheless, responsibility was exactly what Schiller was talking about when he wrote that only the moral person could handle political freedom: only by taking personal responsibility based both on the values and norms of society AND personal emotions, one's autonomous feelings of what is right and wrong, can we enjoy individual freedom and handle political freedom.

At the core of developmental psychology is the same notion, though from a different angle and without the political aspect. By taking responsibility for one part of ourselves, we become free to pursue other things. By learning to control our frustration and anger, we can become good playmates among our peers. By giving up short-term benefits, we can become long-term friends, and by curbing our sexual inclinations, we can become faithful partners who enjoy the freedoms that come with having a spouse. By stepping up to the relationship and taking one's share of the load out of one's own initiative and sense of responsibility, we are each other's freedom.

Bildung is developing this growing sense of responsibility and agency, which allows us to pursue greater degrees of freedom for ourselves and thus to open up for the freedom of others as well. The more we take responsibility due to our own inclinations and agency, the more freedom we can create together with others; the more others take responsibility due to their own inclinations and agency, the more we ourselves can be free.

Through taking responsibility, we become trustworthy, and by maximizing trustworthiness among each other throughout society, we can have trust in society and its institutions. Based on this responsibility, trustworthiness, and trust, we can have non-corrupt bureaucrats and institutions, political freedom, open societies, democracy, and modernity.

The freedom that bildung promotes directly is individual existential freedom. Only as a secondary result does bildung enable political freedom and economic freedom. This makes it hard for many to grasp that bildung is a concept of freedom; freedom they typically understand as political freedom and freedoms such as freedom of speech, freedom of conscience, freedom of assembly, etc., i.e. freedom from the state. Particularly Anglo-Saxons, and especially Americans, tend to be so caught up in these political, liberal concepts of freedom that they are not free to see freedom otherwise. Bildung is freedom but only indirectly relates to the liberal political freedoms, yet the political freedoms would not be there without bildung. Bildung is the freedom that grows from being less controlled by biological instincts, one's emotions, the moral voice of parents and other adults, and the norms of society. Bildung is not freedom from government or other people, it is autonomy and integration; bildung is freedom in a social and cultural context. It is the inner freedom to act and to do what is right, ethically right, because one feels it is right, seen from an increasing time perspective, and a growing social horizon. The longer the time frame, and the bigger the social circle we can identify with and feel an emotional obligation and responsibility towards, the more we are existentially free to take responsibility for grander things and not feel it as an infringement on our personal freedom. Instead, it is freedom from pettier things.

Developmental psychology talks a lot about consciousness, but what makes the existential difference is conscience. Particularly to one's surroundings. The ability not just to be aware of people and issues in the world, but also to actually feel a responsibility towards them and have the skills to make a difference is what makes a difference. This sense of responsibility is built with bildung, and the competences to do something useful based on one's conscience come with bildung as well.

If we look at the words re-spons-ibility, con-science, and con-sciousness, the etymologies of the words tell us why bildung is key.

Re-spons-ibility has at its core 'spons,' which comes from Latin *spondeo*, which means *I promise;* 're-' means that there is a bounce-back or reciprocity, and '–ibility' is basically ability, i.e. a power or capacity. So, responsibility means the capacity to promise mutuality and keep that promise.

Con-science comes from Latin *con,* which means *with*, and *scio,* which means *I know*, and it is, of course the same root as in **con-scious-ness.** So, if both words mean some version of *I-with-know* or *I-co-*

know, what is the significant difference between consciousness and con-science? The ending *–ness* in con-scious-ness indicates that it is a state, a condition, whereas the ending *-ience* indicates an action, something one is actively doing. Consciousness thus is 'what am I capable of knowing,' whereas conscience is 'how am I responding'—which links us straight back to responsibility.

Consciousness says nothing about our impact on the world, it stays within our mind; conscience is a calling, a relationship to others and to the rest of the world, it is a sensibility towards the unspoken condition that lies at the core of all human relationships: I am because you are. My humanity emerges through others seeing me and me seeing and relating to them. You are, because I am, and I must not do you harm. I may accidentally hurt you, but it is my responsibility that I do not; it is my con-science that calls me to use my conscious knowledge and apply it so that I always do my best to preserve the dignity in the situation for both of us—and to take responsibility for the wellbeing of the world around me.

Growing this inner calling, the conscience, the responsibility, and the consciousness is bildung. Increased consciousness allows us to be aware of still bigger chunks of the world and to understand more details. Increased sense of responsibility allows us to give bigger promises to the world. Increased conscience calls us to keep our promises and to make a difference. Bildung is all of that plus the knowledge and skills to engage properly. Hence, also the need for formal education so that one has the skills and the link between formal education and the ability to develop the calling—and not least: the deep emotional satisfaction when we respond to our inner calling. Conscience makes a difference in the world as does responsibility; consciousness in itself does not.

This existential freedom and sense of responsibility and our turning it into daily action is how we build trust. Trust is the flipside of respon-sibility, which is the product of increased existential freedom and bildung. Bildung that stirs our emotions through aesthetics, through grand narratives and art can move us and wake up our conscience and call us to action. This was the inner mechanism that shaped the Nordics. With increasingly complex societies, technologies, and global problems, we need this ability more than ever.

Nationalism, patriotism and national chauvinism

Romantic Nationalism evolved from the *Sturm und Drang* and Idealism of the German bildung philosophers, and it emerged from the access to newspapers, which gave the reading bourgeoisie a sense of what was going on elsewhere in their country. As the feudal societies with their layered estates were replaced by nation states with political freedom and democracy, creating national awareness and a sense of peoplehood throughout the population was essential.

Democracy and nationalism in Denmark, the sense of being Danish, exploded with the two wars in 1848 and 1864, and as Danes we have indulged ourselves in Danishness ever since. One could argue that the only reason our nationalism has not caused our neighboring countries any trouble is that Denmark is tiny and weak. That explanation may be true, but two other border issues tell a different story.

The first Danish non-threatening-nationalism border story regards the border with Germany, the very same border that ignited Danish nationalism in the first place. After WWI (in which Denmark did not participate), Denmark could have claimed both Schleswig and Holstein, and there was a chance Denmark could have gotten them, but something else happened. Denmark only wanted the area where people felt and identified as Danish, hence there was a referendum, the Schleswig-Holsteiners voted, and the border was drawn according to the German and Danish sense of self. There is a Danish minority on the German side and a German minority on the Danish side of the border, and for a couple of generations German and Danish families did not mix. Today, people belonging to the minorities on either side of the border tend to consider themselves both German and Danish, and there is a common 'border land identity' also among people belonging to the two majorities. 2020 is the 100th anniversary of the current border, which is celebrated on both sides.

The other Danish non-threatening-nationalism border story regards Iceland, which; belonged to Denmark, gained its own constitution in 1874, was granted independence under the Danish monarchy in 1918, and while Denmark was occupied by the Nazis (1940-1945), declared itself a republic in 1944. After the war, the Danish answer was not to send the navy, invade Reykjavik and kill the rebels. It was more like "Oh well, OK, then;" the Danish and Icelandic separation has been peaceful, and the common historical roots are intact..

With mass immigration, however, Danish nationalism has taken a chauvinistic form that matches nationalism as it is usually perceived.

Democracy and peoplehood

In order to deal with globalization and migration and to secure social calm, we need a more nuanced understanding of nationalism and peoplehood than is currently the case among many.

We would not have had functioning modern democracies in the West, had our ancestors not developed strong national identities around shared history, language, culture, folklore, and overall narratives about being a people, i.e., had they not produced and promoted a shared symbolic world and shared meaning-making. The reason we are willing to pay taxes to cover the education, healthcare, defense, roads, courthouses, public parks, police, garbage collection, etc. of millions of complete strangers is that we share a narrative as a nation and the spirit that this creates. Through this narrative, we experience a sense of peoplehood, we share meaning-making, we use the same symbols in the same way, and we feel a sense of shared fate.

If this sense of peoplehood breaks down, our democracy and open society will break down too.

Part of the significance of the nation state and why we need it as a sovereign political entity, is that it is the biggest legal entity where most people can speak their mother tongue. It is thus also the biggest democratic entity, in which most people can speak, work, organize themselves, debate, and have influence speaking that mother tongue.

The fact that we can do this, though, is also the product of a deliberate political effort by nation states to homogenize the language. France, for instance, used to have several distinct languages such as Breton, Limousin, and Gascon, but since the French Revolution and particularly with public schools from the 1880s and onwards, other languages than French have been marginalized if not deliberately sought eradicated. The United Kingdom is actually four peoples or nations: England, Scotland, Wales, and Northern Ireland, each with their own language and sense of peoplehood but united in a kingdom, hence the name, and all of them speaking English.

In nation states where the population does not share a mother tongue, democracies tend to be weak; how can there be a meaningful democratic debate, if people cannot communicate fluently and in a nuanced manner about complicated and important matters? Unless the state is willing to pay what it takes for everybody to be bilingual and share at least one common language due to education, then democracy and political stability fare a rocky road. India has managed to unite the country through English, South Africa is trying the same, but the proficiency level is not high throughout the population; both countries have struggling democracies. In Uganda, English is the official language, but many adults barely speak it; Uganda is formally a democracy, but in reality, is becoming a dictatorship. Belgium is more or less split between two peoples: in the north, the Protestant Flemish who speak Dutch (59%), and in the south, the Catholic Walloons who speak French (40%); (there is also a small German-speaking population (1%) bordering Germany in the east). A few years back, the country went without a government for 535 days.

People from English speaking countries can travel to most of the world and get by in English, but migrating and settling in another country, even if people there also speak English as their first language, does not necessarily mean that one participates in all the meaning-making, the symbolic world of that place and the narratives holding that country together. Becoming fully integrated into another nation than the one where one was born and grew up, means learning the language and picking up the spirit, i.e. sharing the symbolic world and making the narratives of that place one's own. This does not mean that one cannot be a fully responsible and loyal citizen who keeps the laws of the land, who pays taxes, who is a great colleague and friend, who contributes to the local community etc. without that level of cultural integration. It just means that the more one does keep the law of the land, joins the culture and plays also by the unspoken rules, contributes, and learns the history and the narratives, the more one takes up the spirit and becomes one of the people. Most Americans moving to India would have few problems intellectually understanding what went on around them, but getting the 'Indian spirit'? That would probably take a while.

A misconception that many non-migrants suffer from is that one can only have one culture, one 'spirit;' one can only be mono-cultural on the inside; to some extent, this was what folk-bildung 1.0 promoted. But this is exactly what the concept of the *bildungs-reise,* the bildung journey challenges: by migrating and living in a foreign culture, our consciousness evolves; to some extent folk-bildung 2.0, the Cultural Radicalism, grasped this, or rather: it came halfway to understanding that. Cultural Radicalism managed to promote an outside-in look on one's first culture and spirit, but it did not promote acquiring more than one culture and along with that acquiring a double spirit, so to speak. It never figured out the value of being bi- or multi-cultural on the inside. Folk-bildung 2.0 did not realize that one can harbor more than one spirit, one epistemology; one can be meaning-making in more than one language and one symbolic world, one can have double consciousness—or triple or more.

It was the American sociologist, historian and civil rights activist Willian Edward Burghardt Du Bois 1868-1963) who invented the term 'double consciousness,' and it is described by British historian Paul Gilroy (b. 1956), in his book *The Black Atlantic—Modernity and Double Consciousness* from 1993. Here Gilroy explores black identity in the aftermath of the trans-Atlantic slave trade, i.e. among people of African descent in the Caribbean and Caribbean minorities in the countries surrounding the Atlantic Ocean. He also looks at double consciousness among other minorities, particularly the Jews. What he explores is how belonging to a minority and thus constantly having to see oneself in relation to a majority culture brings forth a heightened self- and cultural awareness, a double consciousness. Apart from the degrees of oppression and prejudices coming from the majority, double consciousness entails a frustration that emerges from being surrounded by a mono-cultural culture that cannot grasp the richer consciousness of the minorities.

In a globalized, post-industrial, digitized world where we all, one way or the other, will encounter or be migrants who bring along another epistemology, another cultural frame of mind, and where we need functioning democratic nation states inhabited by citizens who share a sense of peoplehood, we need folk-bildung 3.0 that allows us to develop double consciousness and to rethink nationalism. We need to make the local 'spirit' accessible to newcomers, and we need to make ourselves newcomers somewhere.

Rethinking nationalism

In *The Nordic Secret*, my colleague Tomas Björkman and I suggested that we redefine nationalism and patriotism in the following way and add a third concept: national chauvinism:

- **Nationalism**, according to this new definition, is a cultural process that is the fundament of a thriving nation-state democracy. National solidarity and sense of belonging must be cultivated with folk-bildung, overall bildung, and formal education and by practicing and renewing the cultural heritage. Any immigrant who integrates well into their new country can become a nationalist in that culture, and as individuals, we can be nationalists in more than one country. Nationalism is how we identify with any nation state and its people, it is open to newcomers, and nationalism is necessary if we are to trust each other enough to pay taxes and to feel a sense of duty towards shared institutions. Nationalism in this sense is *inclusive* and an *extension* of our sense of belonging to a larger group than our family, village, or the people who share our lifestyle, culture, and values. Without this type of belonging and nationalism, we cannot function as democratic nation states.

- **Patriotism** derives its name from *pater*, i.e. father, and it refers to our ancestors and the fatherland, our *patria*. Children of immigrants may have two *patriae* because they grew up in one country and their parents in another, so they have roots in two places, but generally, most people only have one patria, and it is not something one can do much about. In this sense, patriotism is *exclusive* where nationalism as defined above is *inclusive*; patriotism leaves us emotionally and culturally deeper embedded in one place only.

- **National chauvinism** is nationalism and patriotism gone awry. It has its roots in a mindset of 'us versus them' and where *We* are dependent on *Them* in order to define ourselves. Neither nationalism nor patriotism, as defined above, sees a need for this 'Other' in order for the sense of belonging and collective self to evolve. Patriots can gather around shared heritage, nationalists can gather around renewing that heritage and inviting newcomers into it. It is the chauvinism in national chauvinism that is the problem, and it shares that problem with all other kinds of chauvinism.

This redefinition, to some extent, switches the meaning of nationalism and patriotism the way most people, including political scientists, use the terms today, so creating this new understanding will not be without its challenges. But it makes more sense to see patriotism as the vertical root down into the family-line and place and its anchored history, and nationalism as the horizontal network of meaning-making that regards and includes everybody in the nation now who wants to identify with it and to belong to it. Redefining the words and our understanding like this gives a number of opportunities for creating stable and culturally coherent societies in a time of great changes and migration.

Nationalism as defined above, allows us to be proud, embedded, connected, and committed at the national level as a people and to invite others to join. There should be absolutely no shame in shamelessly celebrating the cultural heritage of a place as long as everybody who wants to join the celebrations are welcome and as long as it does not include neighbor or minority bashing.

Rethinking rethinking nationalism

Shamelessly promoting such senses of peoplehood poses, of course, a huge challenge for nations that consist of more peoples, particularly if one or more ethnic groups have a history of persecuting one or more other ethnic groups. The traditional way to create a coherent nation has been to try to annihilate non-majority language, spirit, epistemology, lore, narrative, cultural heritage, etc. and, eventually, the people carrying these in order to homogenize the nation, its people and its spirit.

To solve this Gordian knot of national cohesion and peoplehood diversity within the same democratic political system, we ought to find developmental psychology, bildung philosophy, the understanding of double consciousness, and folk-bildung useful.

It is perfectly understandable according to both developmental psychology and bildung philosophy that in our formative years, we need a strong, easily recognizable, and culturally coherent We in order to become self-governing; what Schiller called Rational Person, and Pestalozzi called Civic Bildung. It is part of the juvenile mind that we need 'The Bad Other,' the Them versus Us, in order to form our own sense of belonging and solidarity. We are biologically primed to look for enemy tribes in order to be able to identify and protect our own. Part of transitioning from child to adult in pre-historic indigenous societies was, depending on population density and on the part of the men, to become one of the warriors. Transitioning from the self-consolidating mind of the big child to the self-governing mind of the adult means that we are emotionally rewarded when, together with members of our in-group, we despise an out-group.

This sense of 'Us versus Them' is seen in every old John Wayne movie where the "good" settlers are attacked by the "evil" Indians (sic!), and in the many Hollywood action movies where some generic Arab is the terrorist. It is in the American gun debate where many understand the world as populated by "good guys and bad guys;" i.e. "The best response to a bad guy with a gun is a good guy with a gun." It is in the European "anti-fascist" left that explicitly defines itself based on what it claims not to be—while adhering to the exact same violence, black-red-white aesthetics and masked anonymity as the fascists they claim to be against. It is seen in the identitarian, national chauvinist movements, in identity politics, in radical feminism, among incels who dehumanize women, and among the young people who join Daesh/ISIS and who went to Syria to fight for the Caliphate. It is also seen in hooliganism, homophobia, islamophobia, anti-Semitism, anti-Zionism, and in the Old Testament when it tells the Israelites to eliminate the Canaanites, in the Quran when it tells Muslims to fight non-believers, and in Christendom when it keeps blaming the Jews for killing Jesus.

All of the above show how demonizing The Other is a common way of producing self-governing members of in-groups, be it a pre-modern religion, a modern nation, or a post-modern movement on college campuses. What is common across time is that this Us versus Them mode of thinking appeals to adolescents. It makes it attractive to shed their self-consolidating childhood skin and emerge as a self-governing young adult who gives him-, her- or zir-self fully away to the norms and values of their 'we-are-the-good-guys in-group.'

What is unique in our time is that since WWII and the UN Declaration of Human Rights, we no longer accept this kind of dehumanizing tribal thinking at the state level. At least not if we are a democratic nation state with self-respect and a functioning school system.

Four kinds of nationalism

If we do like Herder'and look at nation-states as we do people and distinguish between self-consolidating, self-governing, self-authoring, and self-transforming nation-states and collective senses of self, we can nuance nationalism even further.

Self-consolidating nationalism is national chauvinism classic: We are better that You and more entitled to natural resources, political dominance, or whatever makes us feel great, war included.

Self-governing nationalism is outwardly peaceful but inwardly xenophobic. The days of questioning the sovereignty of other nation-states are over, but we are insecure as a people and need to homogenize the population internally in order to feel safe internally.

Self-authoring nationalism is self-confident about its historical and cultural roots, enjoys its uniqueness and cultural heritage, does not mind flashing it from time to time, but is also curious about the cultures of other peoples and nations. The self-authoring nationalism is promoted by boosting the authoring, i.e. the cultural production, the cultural institutions, the heritage that is there, and by challenging it through new input, questioning it and playing around with it.

Self-transforming nationalism is so self-confident it can assist other nationalisms in other nations becoming self-authoring. In some respects, this was what the Marshall Plan did to Europe after WWII: A massive investment in democratization, industry, education, and to some extent culture. Europe, the old Lady, needed recovery, and Mr. Marshall realized she would remain a threat to everybody, not least herself, if nobody showed her a bit of love and courtesy.

Self-consolidating nationalism was how Denmark and Bismarck fought over Schleswig-Holstein, and it is how many if not most modern nation-states were born. Self-governing nationalism is Brexit: the UK has matured beyond starting a war, but not yet with enough imagination to be self-authoring within the EU. As modern, democratic societies, we have come to expect the tolerance and maturity of self-authoring from our political leadership and from our nation-states as such, and when peoples and their states cannot muster that, it becomes a sorry spectacle. As self-authoring, be it as individuals, as groups, as peoples, or as nation-states, we know who we are and who we ought to be from a moral perspective, and we do not need an enemy or a 'The Other' in order to figure out who we are. We are authoring our own story. As self-authoring nation states, we no longer need neighboring countries as a mirror, and we can appreciate the inner diversity and complexity provided by cultural and religious minorities. At least, so it is when we are at our best.

Immigration

Mass-immigration is threatening this self-authoring nationalism if we do not keep up the bildung effort, invest in our culture, and make it visible and accessible. If there is not a shared epistemology and shared moral norms that more or less everybody willingly plays by, misunderstandings arise and anxiety increases. With insufficient bildung, the societal fabric tears apart. Particularly if individuals are self-governing and take their moral guidance from their surroundings, not from their inner, personal moral compass, then a multicultural society isn't just a society struggling with itself, the conflicts in society become inner discomfort in the individual. The self-governing individual's need for in-group loyalty is challenged, and the safest space to run is homogenous groups within the society, i.e. smaller communities and tribes. A self-authoring nation with self-authoring nationalism challenged by immigration runs the risk of becoming not just a self-governing, anxious nation, but a self-consolidating tribal mess, unless we boost the shared meaning-making, i.e. the local culture and epistemology through bildung and folk-bildung.

Multiethnic states

Looking at the nation state from these perspectives opens up two options when it comes to states comprised of more than one people. Either accept that the historical wounds are so deep and painful that staying together is not an option and each people should have their own state, or the two or more peoples are so intricately mixed that there is a need for developing a new, shared narrative regarding that and becoming a self-authoring nation on those terms.

India is an example of both: with regards to Pakistan and Bangladesh, two regions got their own state; with regards to the rest of India, a modern Indian sense of peoplehood has been in the making since Gandhi, and his fellow countrymen and –women managed to kick out the British. That was in 1947, and all three countries, India, Pakistan and Bangladesh, are still struggling to find out what it means to be a people and a nation state with large ethnic and religious minorities.

A nation state that remained together despite a recent genocide is Rwanda. The country is deliberately creating a new Rwandan narrative and a sense of shared identity. Among other things, all Rwandans participate in cleaning the streets one Saturday every month.

Staying together as a nation of more than one people is hard. South Africa did not have any other option than staying together after the end of Apartheid, and the country created a deliberate process of truth and reconciliation. This started out as an amazing process and a unique and impressive narrative. According to the constitution, The Republic of South Africa is one, sovereign, democratic state founded on the values of equality and the advancement of human rights and freedoms, but it has not invested in promoting them. They spilled their story on the floor and are, it seems, back to tearing the country apart.

Self-authoring benefits

According to Schiller, only the moral person, i.e. the self-authoring, can handle political freedom. As self-authoring, one is capable of developing one's own path in life in harmony with one's surroundings based on that inside oneself, which is unique. If peoples and nation-states could do that for themselves—and for the world—what an amazing and rich world we could create.

If peoples and nation-states could even become self-transforming and see their own impact on the world as a whole, and on other peoples and nation-states and if they could thus contribute to creating sustainable economic, political and other development around the globe, that would change our fate as a species. It will also be the only path to avoiding pandemics in the future.

From this perspective, celebrating what is unique about America in America, Denmark in Denmark, and likewise in India, Pakistan, Bangladesh, Brazil, Palestine, Israel, Tibet, China, Vietnam, Turkey, Armenia, Kurdistan, Germany, Belgium, Serbia, Bosnia, Ukraine, Russia, and anywhere else should be praiseworthy in any of those places. It just has to be the open and tolerant, self-authoring, redefined nationalism, not the self-consolidating and self-governing national chauvinism.

The path towards this would have to have at least two tracks:

- an appreciation of individual bildung, emancipation and double consciousness,
- a major investment in folk-bildung everywhere, be it folk-high-schools, community centers, and better primary and secondary schools with much more focus on cultural heritage, narrative, literature, philosophy, languages, history, human rights, new technologies, and global challenges—and question based open conversations.

Preferably, we would all keep pursuing education and bildung until we developed not just self-authoring but also double consciousness through bildung from more than one culture. Such a path would be a school for life.

Promoting nationalism based on this understanding and these goals should have at least the following advantages:

- Millions of people around the globe whose identity is deeply rooted in their sense of peoplehood and/or national belonging can relax: nobody is going to take their culture away from them. Quite the contrary.
- With increased celebration of local culture, we will have access to symbolic worlds with more depth, stronger local flavor, more uniqueness, and rooted in the local flora, fauna, and climate.
- By strengthening that which is local, we can explore and promote indigenous knowledge, culture, and traditions that will allow us to live in harmony with the local nature and thus solve many of our environmental problems.
- With this local depth of culture around the globe, we would have access to more ways of expressing the universal human spirit; we would have a richer meaning-making pool from which to draw lessons about what it means to be human.
- Tourism in neighboring countries would become more interesting, and we can spare the environment from several plane trips.
- As democracies, we can harvest all that wonderful energy that comes from nationalism and channel it towards long-term solutions for our countries.
- With a stronger sense of rootedness and cultural cohesion internally in entities where we can communicate in our mother tongue, we can also start deeper and more meaningful conversations about the future and the challenges from climate change, mass-extinction of species, globalization, AI, surveillance capitalism, pandemics, etc. We can also develop politics that reaches outside our peoples and nation-states. With a sense of cultural rootedness and security, we can get involved in how our nation-state can contribute to solving global problems, how it can become

self-transforming. A strong sense of national and local anchoring makes it less anxiety provoking to face different cultures and embrace even bigger and more abstract communities, such as the global community.

- If national cultural heritage is strengthened, bilingual youth (i.e. typically children of immigrants) become a cultural resource and an asset, not a threat to a weak collective sense of self. With their double consciousness, they have some of the mental complexity we need in order to solve complex global problems.

The danger is not that people love their nation, but the chauvinism that prevents us from loving other nations as well and from harboring that which is different among us within the nation. The danger is that we do not know our own culture well enough to invite others into it.

Circles of belonging

We need self-authoring nationalism in order to sustain our nation-states and to strengthen cultural diversity around the globe, but we need nationalism for another reason too: feeling a sense of belonging in a country, identifying with it and taking responsibility for it is just one instance of identifying and feeling solidarity with people one will never meet. In order to solve global problems created by our lifestyles and consumption but too big for our nation-states to handle individually, we need to develop a sense of solidarity with people around the globe simply because we share a planet. Our consciousness, conscience, solidarity, and responsibility must reach as far as our impact.

From the moment we are born, we have the potential to expand the world to which we relate and for which we can take responsibility. This can be illustrated as Circles of Belonging, beginning with our sense of self and expanding from there:

1. Ego / Self
2. Family 1 (parents and siblings—the family we are born into / raised by)
3. Peer group
4. Family 2 (spouse, children, in-laws—the family we create ourselves)
5. Communities (neighborhood, sports team, colleagues at workplace, house of prayer, etc.)
6. Imagined community (society / country / nation / people // religious denomination)
7. Culture zone
8. Humanity today and universal principles
9. All life on the planet now
10. Life itself and future generations that we will never en-counter

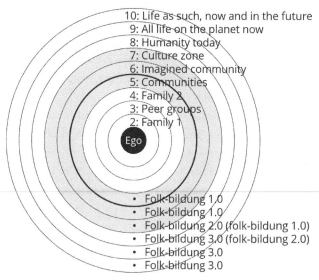

Figure 4: Circles of Belonging

Source: The Nordic Secret

There could be more circles, there could be less; the number is not the point. What matters is that the first entity we feel at home in and responsible for is our body, and then consciousness, conscience, loyalty, solidarity, sense of responsibility, and ability to make a difference expand outwards. The order of the circles illustrates the complexity of the circles and/or the demands they put on us, i.e. they do not necessarily illustrate the exact order in which everybody gains consciousness about them, though there is that tendency. Today's children will most likely develop consciousness regarding the global environment before they develop an understanding and sense of responsibility towards, say, local communities or country. Fundamentally important about all the circles is that we must be conscious about something before we can feel conscience towards it, the conscience must be aroused before loyalty and solidarity can set in and spur responsibility, and we generally must develop an understanding of the system as a whole before we can take responsibility for the whole.

Though the number of circles might be different (one could argue that there should be a circle for 'cities' between communities and nation), the ten circles are not random; each of them represents a different level of complexity and responsibility, and they are very different in character. Skipping a circle or two would typically leave a gap in one's bildung and emotional development.

Circle 1, ourselves, is hardly a circle as such, but our sense of belonging and consciousness emerge in the body, and conscience and responsibility grow from there. Around the age of two, we become self-aware, and the care and attention we have received until then will define much of our emotional development for the rest of our life: attachment, empathy, self-control, the ability to love and trust, loyalty, solidarity, and much more.

Circle 2 is Family 1, the family we are born into and/or raised by. It is the first social entity we learn to identify with; it is the first 'We' that we experience and thus the first 'We versus other people out there' that gives us a sense of identity. With some 50% of all marriages in the West ending in divorce, many children grow up with more than one Family

1 and have to navigate more than one Family 1 We, which can be very challenging if the adults are not careful and protect the children from conflicts of loyalty.

Circle 3, peer-groups, begin to emerge around age 4, and from around age 5, peer-groups gradually begin to replace Family 1 as the social entity from which we take our moral guidance. The big difference between peer-groups and Family 1 is that Family 1 raises us and was already there and had a life of its own before we existed; our peer-groups only exist because we contribute to them and constitute them. Hence, it is important that by age 4, children have learned to control their iimpulses, to behave, and to play with other kids; if they have not reached this level of emotional maturity, other kids will not form peer-groups with them.

Circle 4 is Family 2, the family for which we take responsibility as adults. The committed responsibility towards a family entails the willingness to, from time to time, carry 100% of the load. With divorce and remarriage, many have more than one Family 2.

Circle 5, communities, we typically belong to several social entities in Circle 5, such as a workplace, sports club, local neighborhood, associations, house of prayer, etc. These communities were typically there before we ourselves joined and they will continue after we leave; they therefore typically have formal rules that we need to be able to play by, uphold and eventually be capable of taking responsibility for, particularly if we join the leadership and/or the organization is democratic.

The common denominator for circles of belonging 2-5 is that they are real communities: we relate personally to the people there. In circle 5, we may not know everybody personally, but we know of almost everybody and probably know everybody's face. There is also an actual chance that at some point we will have encountered everybody.

Circles 6-10 are fundamentally different, they are what sociologists and cultural theorists call imagined communities. Imagined communities are characterized by being held together not by personal connections but by narrative and a sense of shared fate, which means that we need to share language and symbols, i.e. meaning-making. It was the historian

Benedict Anderson (1936-2015) who coined the term imagined communities in his book by the same name in 1983.

Circles 6-10 are imagined communities: we can only identify with everybody in these circles if we are educated and have the bildung to do so.

Circle 6 may be nation state / country / people and/or religion, and these are crucial imagined communities. This is where the moral values of society emerge and are negotiated, where language is produced and where artists interpret those values and push the aesthetics, the ethics, and the collective boundaries of meaning-making to their limits in order to express that which the spoken language is not capable of expressing yet. Circle 6 is why we have awe-inspiring temples, synagogues, cathedrals, and mosques. It is why we have the most mesmerizing religious music, and it is why we have civilizations, museums, art museums, historical palaces, squares and ruins, theaters, libraries, and cities worth visiting. Circle 6 produces symbols that connect not just millions of strangers in time but also through time.

Some other communities that may be characterized as imagined communities are class, race, gender, and sexual orientation. They produce language, meaning-making, art, and symbols of their own, but they are dependent on the language and aesthetics of the nation-states within which these identities arise, and they rarely create the kind of social infrastructure that nation-states and religions do, i.e., solidarity based institutions that feed the poor and educate everybody's children. The workers' movements in some places got close at some point, though.

Circle 7 is the culture zone, which does much of what circle 6 does, it just does it in several languages and with a much wider variety of symbols, traditions, and meaning-making, etc. The language and symbols of Circle 6 the individual tends to get from Familiy 1, whereas the language and symbols of Circle 7, we get from education, media and travelling. Few families bring up their children as, say, Africans or Westerners, we would normally bring up children as, say, Bantu, Nigerians or Portuguese. What constitutes a culture zone may vary and depends on the situation. From a Danish perspective, the culture zone could be the Nordics, Europe or the

Judeo-Christian West as a whole; from a Tunisian perspective, it might be Northern Africa, the Arabic world, and the Muslim world.

Circle 8 is humanity, i.e., all living humans and the universal principles that allow us to see all humans as humans and equals. All the previous circles have pitted some sort of Us against some sort of Them; Circle 8 takes us from 'We-excluding-some' to 'We-absolutely-all-of-us.' In order for universal principles to be universal, they must cover all humans, even the ones we do not like at all. This is a hard pill to swallow, because our brains are tribal brains that prefer to mentally organize the world in in-groups and out-groups. With only one giant We, the out-group is missing; there is no way for any human to not qualify for this circle. Circle 8 not only includes all those peoples and other groups we learned to dislike as children when parents and teachers taught us our nation-ality, religion and football team affiliation, it also includes our political opponents and people of all faiths, plus war criminals, terrorists, child molesters, serial killers, school shooters, rapists, and everybody else one might severely detest. Including, had they still been alive, Adolph Hitler and Pol Pot. All 8 billion people soon out there. The principles that we are talking about had a precursor in Persia under the rule of Cyrus, but other than that they were first formulated as universal human rights around the time of the French Revolution. Since then, in the aftermath of the Holocaust, our species created the universal principles that are the UN Universal Declaration of Human Rights; it took us some 6,000 years of written civilization to produce them. Now we need to take responsibility and practice them, and we can only do that if we develop the bildung that allows us to identify with, feel conscience and loyalty towards, and solidarity with all humans. At the end of the day, it is the only way we can fight a pandemic like COVID-19.

Circle 9 is all life, and if we are not conscious about life as such, if we do not feel conscience, loyalty, and solidarity with it, if we do not feel a sense of belonging on the globe as a whole, we cannot take responsibility for it, and we cannot survive. At least not all of us. Life on Earth is in its sixth mass extinction of species, this is caused by humans, and it is not just that certain species will disappear, it is the balance and survival of entire eco-systems that are at stake. Earth is our home, and we are literally burning it down, as the Australian summer 2019-2020 has shown. One major part of the reason we have brought ourselves into this situation is our lack of bildung; we lack the education, enculturation and emotional development that would raise our consciousness to deal with the fact that we are an integral part of all life on the planet; we are not beyond it or above it. We even share the same DNA and RNA. The reason the corona virus spread, is that the cells in our bodies are hijacked to become corona factories. From the basic DNA and RNA molecules in all living cells to the global climate, all life is connected, and our inability to feel it is a disastrous lack of bildung.

Circle 10 are all humans who ever lived and will live plus the planet as a whole, past, present and future. Feeling a sense of belonging, consciousness, conscience, loyalty, solidarity, responsibility, and deep connectedness to everything and everyone in this circle is by all means a spiritual experience, and it probably comes very close to what most spiritual traditions would call enlightenment. It is a sense of connectedness to evolution itself, integrated and embedded in life as a process, in the circles of life, and in the interplay of those circles of life. As with the other circles of belonging, the path to this sense of belonging is bildung. Kohlberg comes close to Circles 8, 9, and 10 in his 6th level of moral reasoning, which is about universal principles and responsibility beyond our own time. Surrendering to this level of consciousness, embeddedness, and understanding of yourself as a vessel permeated by the flow of the universe and time could also be called wisdom and infinite love.

All the circles are equally important

Looking at life from the perspective of the ten Circles of Belonging is daunting, and the temptation to pick one circle and declare it the most important is huge. But that is not how it works; we need all of them; they constitute each other. The world is made up of open, self-organizing, complex systems within open, self-organizing, complex systems; that goes for our societies and groups as well, and it goes for our minds and our bodies, it is just that our bodies are self-organizing according to a genetic code that is our DNA. Each of the circles represents a level of complexity in a self-organizing world of systems within systems, and we cannot single out one level of complexity and call it The Most Important.

Like the layers of ego-development, there is a typical order to a harmonious, individual development towards a still more complex inner world, from the inner circles outwards to the bigger circles. As individuals, we engage in the world based on the core that we have already developed; our sense of belonging and consolidation in the inner circles is what allows us to expand our consciousness, conscience, loyalty, solidarity, sense of responsibility, capabilities, and love beyond our current comfort zone. The circles we have not embraced yet and where we do not yet feel a genuine sense of belonging may seem intimidating, but we can grow throughout life. Not just regarding our emotions and sense of self, the way that developmental psychology describes it, but also regarding the circles with which we identify and to which we feel a sense of belonging.

It may look as if the significance emanates from the center and out, but that is just our personal journey; in reality, each circle holds every circle within it. There is an inwards-outwards dynamic going on all the time, where we as individuals make up groups that take responsibility for their surroundings, and surroundings that provide the foundation for groups and their individuals. There is no up or down in this model. The evolution holds all life, which holds all humans, which uphold culture zones, which harbor peoples and nation states, which define the rights and freedoms of communities, which are the frameworks around families, into which we are born as individuals who can engage outwards via family, peer-groups, communities, and our country towards and with all the circles of belonging.

There is also no conflict between the circles per se. Whatever conflict we may perceive between, say, nation and continent, or humans versus the global environment, it is all in our heads and in inadequate bildung and institutions. There is no inherent conflict between nation-states and human rights, just like there is no conflict between being a daughter, a sister, a mother, a colleague, a citizen, and a devoted Buddhist simultaneously.

A trait of the Circles, though, is that if a conflict arises among individuals or groups within a circle, the bigger circle around it is typically the authority we tend to seek if we do not want to use violence. If children cannot resolve their own conflicts, they fight or go to their parents. If two spouses cannot get along, they fight or seek advice in their community, and if that does not work, they go to the courts of the nation. When political leaders decided in the aftermath of WWI that there should be no more war, they created the League of Nations. When that failed, WWII broke out, and when political leaders decided in the aftermath of that war that there should be war no more, they created the United Nations, and the United Nations created the Universal Declaration of Human Rights. Whenever we have a conflict as individuals with our nation-state, or two nation-states with each other, this is the authority to which we can appeal. Or at least: that was what the UN was set up to do; when the nation-states choose not to uphold the UN and the principles behind the UN, and the UN does not apply its own principles universally, the UN cannot fulfill its mission. When the European nation-states decided that there should be no more wars in Europe, we created a political power that represented the culture zone, and over the course of two generations we created the EU—and enjoyed peace.

What we have been poor at is providing the education and bildung that allows all of us to find all ten circles meaningful and important, and to take it upon ourselves to support and carry them.

Folk-bildung 1.0, 2.0 and 3.0

If we look at the Danish folk-high-schools and folk-bildung 1.0 from the perspective of the Circles of Belonging, what the schools managed to do 150 years ago and onwards, was to lift the rural youth from Circle 5 out into the 6th Circle of Belonging: the imagined community of people, nation state and Christendom. Before going to one of the schools, the young people of the 1860s would have been conscious about being Danish and

Christian, but it would have been intangible and abstract, and they would most likely have identified with their local village, their parish or just their parents' farm. At the folk-high-schools, they developed a conscience, a sense of loyalty and solidarity, and responsibility towards Denmark, and towards their personal faith, plus a new kind of personal responsibility towards the inner circles of family, peers and local community. They were also made conscious about their culture zone, particularly the Nordics; in some schools, they even learned Icelandic in order to be able to read the Icelandic sagas in the original language.

If we then combine the Circles of Belonging with Kegan's five phases or layers and Schillers three phases of bildung, we can be even more specific about what the folk-high-schools and other folk-bildung 1.0 did: Regarding the real communities, i.e., circles 2-5, the youngsters became self-authoring, Moral Persons. They learned to figure out for themselves what was right or wrong. Regarding the imagined communities, which back then meant just Circles 6 and 7, the picture is less clear. The students were internalizing the norms of Danish society and Christendom to become self-governing Christian Danes; there was no doubt about the wonderfulness of Denmark and Evangelical Lutheranism. Yet, there was freedom of thought, of discussion, of speech, and of doubt and questions of any kind; anything and everything could be discussed. Freedom for Loke as well as for Thor. Opening the mind while remaining a loyal and responsible citizen was the goal.

Folk-bildung 2.0, Cultural Radicalism, its poetry, satire, design, and overall aesthetics, did what it could to extend people's consciousness beyond the 6th Circle of Belonging to the culture zone and to humanity as a whole; Circles 7 and 8. Unfortunately, the Cultural Radicals did so by belittling the nation-state; they saw (and generally still see) it as a relic of the past.

Today we need education and a folk-bildung 3.0, which can help all of us develop a sense of belonging and responsibility, self-governing and then self-authoring, and to become a Moral Person, in all ten Circles, preferably quickly.

The Bildung Rose

Given the complexity of today's society, there is an enormous challenge with regards to giving everybody the necessary education and scaffold the bildung that would allow everybody to thrive. The Bildung Rose is a philosophy for connecting our inner worlds to the society in which we grow up and where we ought to thrive throughout life. How much of my society do I understand? The model also serves as an analytical tool regarding societal development: How internally balanced, cooperative, and coherent is any given society?

The idea behind the Bildung Rose is to describe societies in such a way that we can have a qualified conversation about what kind of knowledge and understanding people in any given society need, and this model should be applicable to all societies, irrespectively of complexity, economic development, cultural code, etc.

The Bildung Rose, therefore, is built on the claim that from the early hunter-gatherers to today, all functioning societies have had the seven domains or sub-systems listed below. All functioning societies can be described through these seven domains, and in order to thrive in their society, individuals need to understand the basics of all seven domains the way they are in their society, and they must have the freedom to influence all of them through participation if they so wish:

- **Production**
- **Technology**
- **Factual knowledge/science**
- **Ethics** (underlying principles that can give directions in unfamiliar situations)
- **Narrative** (history, religion and moral values that give directions in familiar situations)
- **Aesthetics** (traditional culture, pop-culture, and the arts)
- **Political power** (religious, democratic, authoritarian, oligarchy, or other)

In the Bildung Rose, the political power is at the center with the six other domains as its 'petals':

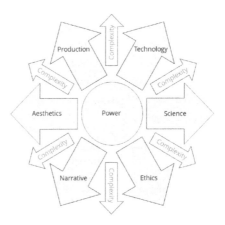

Figure 5: The Bildung Rose

The reason nature does not have a domain of its own is that society and thus the seven domains of the Bildung Rose are a part of human life, which is a part of nature; nature is the foundation for all of the domains, which is what the Circles of Belonging show.

The seven domains of the Bildung Rose are, of course, very different in societies of different sizes and complexity. Historically, over time, as societies grew in size and the number of inhabitants, the domains specialized, diversified, and increasingly became individual sub-systems. In a hunter-gatherer society, the seven domains are inseparable, as narrative (myth) contains the knowledge ("science") necessary to find food (production) and to survive. In the Bronze Age, artisans (production) increasingly specialized, and priests (narrative) became a caste of their own. What characterized the Renaissance in the West was the separation of narrative (church) and science, and during the Enlightenment, the West went through the separation of narrative (church) and political power. Throughout history, this increase in the autonomy of the domains turned them into separate sub-systems with institutions, sub-sub-systems, and complexity of their own. This development was made possible by increasingly sophisticated communication technologies that could keep still larger societies together, and it was paralleled by an increasing autonomy of the individual and thus an increasing need for formal education and bildung in order for people to cope.

By comparing the domains of hunter-gatherer tribes and (post)modern, democratic, industrialized nation-states, the differences in complexity between them stand out. It also shows the complexities that humans of our era have to deal with:

	Hunter-gatherers	Modern, democratic, industrialized nation-states
Production	Hunting, fishing, picking fruits, digging for tubers	Housing, agriculture, factories, crafts, means of transfer (money), banks / financial products, infrastructure, etc.
Technology	Stone axes & knives, snares, bows & arrows	Writing, printing, radio, television, phones, machinery, cars, computers, software, robots, internet, mechanical tools, new means of transfer; crypto currencies etc.
Knowledge	Information passed on orally through myths and rituals	Math, physics, natural sciences, social sciences, economic theory, liberal arts, journalism; various scientific processes of data collection, falsification, peer-reviews etc.
Ethics	Not explicit; by intuition *	Philosophical tradition, formal logic, critical thinking, the process of exploring the highest ethical principles possible, humanism, UN Universal Declaration of Human Rights
Narrative	Stories and mythology	History, religious heritage, political ideology, national identity, and various types of lore and tradition
Aesthetics	Inherited and uniform	Folklore heritage, pop-culture, avant-garde art, individual expression, multicultural input, and mixes thereof
Power	Shamans and wise elders	Municipality & state democracy, courts, police, army, EU, multilateral institutions and treaties, tech giants etc.

Table 3: Bildung Rose domains then and now

* Exploring the universal principles behind the morals of a society demands a level of abstraction that only emerges with writing. Since hunter-gatherer cultures are oral, it is unlikely that hunter-gatherers would have managed to express their ethics.

We are still born with 'hunter-gatherer brains' and are thus biologically prepared to be born into the Stone Age. Only through education, enculturation, life experience, and our moral and emotional development, i.e. bildung, can we come to understand and handle the complexities of our society. This was also the case in pre-historic indigenous and pre-modern societies, but it is particularly the case in modern, postmodern and metamodern societies. Which means that today, the need for formal education, schools, cultural venues, literature, libraries, and all aspects of bildung is overwhelming if everybody is to understand and be able to take responsibility for their society in any democratic way or form.

Schools and folk-bildung

The Bildung Rose shows what our school systems ought to provide and what the folk-high-schools in Denmark did provide in the 1860s and onwards: basic knowledge in all domains matching the development of the surrounding society.

The folk-high-schools did not have this Rose as a checklist, and yet they managed to cover all the domains. Or, at least they did so for the first 100 years; the Danish folk-high-schools today are generally not up to speed regarding production, technological development, science, and the changes in power structures caused by new technologies, and they are increasingly ignoring narrative and barely teach any history. The aesthetics and ethics tend to be relatively strong, though, and in some schools they focus on sustainable production. But for 100 years, the folk-high-schools covered the full Rose:

The young farmhands and –girls of the late 1800s learned how to improve the production on their farms, and they learned the latest agricultural technologies and techniques, among them how to work with fermentation and make better cheeses and beer. They learned about the latest science and improved their skills in reading, writing, and math.

As for ethics, some schools may have taught philosophy as such and may have had the students read some of the philosophical classics. Generally, though, they just practiced the Socratic method: questions, discussions, doubting, challenging the thoughts and ideas of each other and even of the teachers; learning to think for oneself and finding out why one had the moral values one did.

The trademark of the early folk-high-schools was the narratives. This was what Grundtvig and Kold saw before they even knew what a folk-high-school was going to be like. Great stories, national history, world history, the grand narratives of the Norse mythology, the Greek and Roman mythologies, the Icelandic Sagas, Beowulf, and the stories of the Bible. Central in the folk-high-schools were the meaning-making and moral struggles handed down to us since the dawn of civilization, the spirit, and thus the input for the ethics questions, the discussions, the doubts, the challenging thoughts, and for making up one's own mind about the world.

The schools were frugal, but they were also beautiful. As the folk-high-school movement built momentum and attracted funding, the willingness to lift the spirit of the young students through art and the best artisanship available produced some amazing buildings. Particularly the lecture halls were designed and decorated as if to tell the youngsters: We see the best in you, now you develop it and show it to the world!

The core of the Bildung Rose is power, i.e., in society, the political power. The folk-high-schools were explicitly aware that they should not tell their students what their political viewpoints should be. Instead, they taught the students simple political science, had politicians speak at the schools, and took the students to political meetings; all for the sake of letting the young people make up their own mind regarding politics. What we should assume, though, is that their discussions focused on what kind of politics would serve the country as a whole, not just the individual voter. Politics should serve Denmark, not be about "What's in it for me?" The aim would have to be Kohlberg's level 4 and 5: "Will this serve societal structures?" and "Does this serve everybody and the bigger picture?".

The bildung Rose and the individual

The bildung Rose also illustrates what needs to be present in our individual lives, if we are to be appropriately meaning-making in our society and to take responsibility as citizens. If we do not grasp what is going on in all the domains, we are not empowered. If we cannot contribute to the production and provide for ourselves; if we cannot use the latest technology appropriately; if we cannot make decisions based on the latest science; if we cannot develop ethics that allow us to make appropriate choices in unfamiliar situations; if we cannot pass on our cultural heritage; if we cannot appreciate the arts and aesthetics that expand the collective symbolic world—then we cannot remain in power over our own life.

When we apply the bildung Rose like this, not to society, but to the individual, the power in the middle represents the power over self. The emotional development, the ego-development, or the bildung from Physical/Emotional Person via Rational Person to Moral Person that Schiller wrote about. Sufficient knowledge and emotional development must go hand in hand.

A claim often made against bildung is that bildung did not prevent nazism, WWII and the Holocaust. German culture was the cradle of *Bildung*, so many people had *Bildung* and some top Nazis were among the best educated; they knew history, art, philosophy, and science, and enjoyed classical music. One of the greatest German philosophers of the time, Martin Heidegger, was even a member of the Nazi party from May 1933 until the end of the war. How could they? And how can anybody claim that bildung will make a difference with regards to the human soul and our ability to create, uphold, and protect democracy?

The Bildung Rose in combination with the folk-high-schools gives us an answer. Just knowing, intellectually, everything about production, technology, science, ethics, history & religion, aesthetics, and politics is not enough; that is not bildung. Bildung is the process that takes place when the content is discussed, challenged, doubted, explored with others, and when one realizes that one has suffered from a misconception because one did not see the full picture, or because one was misinformed. These pushbacks, these experiences of smaller or larger instances of "Jeez, what an idiot I have been!" is a crucial part of bildung.

A transition must take place in the individual in order for it to be bildung; merely knowing more is not enough. Schiller's two transitions of bildung can be summed up like this:

- **Emotional / Natural Person / self-consolidating**
- **Transition away from self-consolidating, Emotional / Natural Person**, being calmed down by aesthetics and becoming aligned with society.
  - **Rational Person / self-governing**
- **Transition away from self-governing, Rational Person**, being invigorated by aesthetics, waking up, feeling one's feelings again, and gaining the personal courage, strength, and enthusiasm that makes a difference.
  - **Moral Person / self-authoring**

The Nazis definitely missed the second transition and perhaps they even missed the first. Or what most likely happened was: they were socialized and came of age as self-governing according to the moral norms of the militaristic, patriarchal, Prussian authoritarianism that defined Germany before the Weimar Republic, and when the Republic was supposed to be a modern, open democracy, they could not handle it. They could not change their worldview, they could not learn to self-govern according to modernity and democracy, and they could not make the transition to self-authoring either. Instead, they insisted on self-governing according to the old norms, developed aesthetics that were literally made to make everybody march in unison, and created a political system that was willing to use any kind of violence to maintain a bygone era, militaristic, patriarchal, Prussian authoritarianism at any cost. While the rest of Europe and the US moved on to modernity and democracy, Germany (and Italy) tried to remain in the past.

The German Jewish philosopher and psychologist Erich Fromm, who explored moral aloneness and our need for a shared symbolic world, described this psychological lack of development as an *Escape from Freedom*, which is also the title of his book from 1941.

In other words: top Nazis may have had the finest education in some or all of the seven domains, even regarding the moral norms of their fatherland and in the arts, but they did not have bildung. A historical fact adds weight to this suggestion: in 1871, Bismarck shut down the workers' bildung associations in Prussia for fear of revolution; the only education the workers were allowed to continue was the upgrading of their professional skills and lectures of non-political cultural content. And—this is the interesting part—Q & A's after the lectures were forbidden. No discussions were allowed; the audience had to go straight home right away. Prussian values did not include questioning authorities.

Being a team player or not

The Bildung Rose shows seven domains that need to be in balance in order for our societies and the humans in them to thrive.

As we as individuals get an education and find a profession, we will be spending a huge part of our life, typically in just one of the domains. That is how we become experts, climb the career ladder, and contribute to the constant development of the domain we are in—and doing so, we contribute to further specialization within the domain. Specialization and diversification within the domains is generally an advantage because it means a greater diversity of output, higher quality of the contributions of each domain to society, and better use of resources.

Specialization and diversification may also have the opposite consequences, though, if the increased complexity in one domain does not match the development of the rest of society. If one or two domains 'take off' and become much more complex than the rest of society. If they do not co-evolve with the rest of society, or if they do not allow the other domains to evolve and become more complex as well, they can tear society apart. Each domain has the potential to disconnect from the rest and stop being a team player:

- **Production** can become cynical, abusive, and exploitative (slavery, oil spills, felling pristine forests, pollution in general, climate change etc.).
- **Technology** can disrupt societal structures and institutions (Gutenberg's printing press, Amazon disrupting local commerce etc.).
- **Science** can become arrogant (scientists just writing for other scientists), it can undermine the current narrative holding society together (Darwin), and it can become scientism that dismisses all other aspects of life.
- **Ethics** that call for hitherto unknown levels of personal freedom and responsibility can challenge the moral values represented by narrative and thereby cause anxiety (what most likely happened to traditionally-minded Germans who preferred Prussian authoritarianism to democracy and freedom).
- **Narrative** can become narrow-minded and prevent necessary development (Saudi Arabia, Iran), and it can evolve into a political ideology that becomes dogmatic and totalitarian when it cannot tolerate contradicting isms (Nazism, fascism, communism).
- **Aesthetics** can become art that tears the symbolic fabric apart and causes confusion (Goethe, Schiller, Pablo Picasso, Salvador Dali, Nina Simone, Beatles, Quinten Tarantino etc.), and aesthetics can be the commercial bling that lures us into complacency and instant pleasure and away from emancipation and political responsibility.
- **Power** may be abusive and controlling. Power may be hijacked by or take over one or two of the other domains, by which it will become abusive and controlling on behalf of that one or those two domain(s) (China's massive abuse of its own population through the application of surveillance technology and the system of Sesame Credits).

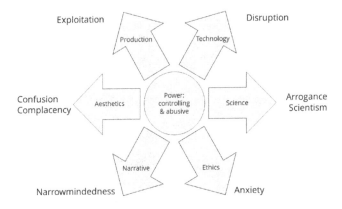

Figure 6: Bildung Rose extremes

All domains can become a threat to society as a whole whenever they do not accept and take into account the rest of society and input/ viewpoints from the other domains. When a domain stops appreciating the other six domains or stops collaborating with them, each domain has the power to ruin society, some domains more than others, depending on the society. Even ethics can do this: more freedom and responsibility than people can handle with the bildung they have available may cause a longing for simpler principles, which may lead to a longing for authoritarian, totalitarian implementation of such simpler ethics.

If, on the other hand, people want to contribute to the balanced, stable and peaceful development of their society, they must reach out to the other domains, particularly the domain 'across the aisle.'

This is important not least regarding the top and bottom of the model. They represent the pragmatic, concrete material here and now (top) and the long-term perspectives, the spirit and the existential foundation (bottom):

What is physically possible
here and now

What might be possible

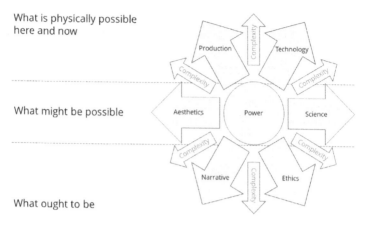

What ought to be

Figure 7: Bildung Rose top and bottom

In general, though, our systems in modern society are not set up for this collaboration and it requires a substantial amount of both knowledge about the other domains and personal (self-authoring) courage and determination to reach across. Particularly if one wants one's organization to do it too, which is necessary if it is to have any impact.

Using the Bildung Rose as a guiding tool, it is easy to see how collaboration across the aisle / across the Rose may benefit everybody:

- When production has ethics, and ethics deliberately assists commerce and production, they can produce sustainable prosperity.
- When narrative (particularly in the shape of religion) recognizes that societies grow and put more demands on us as technologies can hold more people together, and that our need for education and understanding thus evolves, then narrative can realize that it must evolve as well. It must update its morals towards more freedom and responsibility and start exploring new ethics. Technology similarly has to pay attention to the narratives and morals that keep society together and secure meaningful social peace. Together,

narrative and tech can create meaningful and purposeful development.

- When science and aesthetics (pop-culture as well as the arts) collaborate, they can produce understanding; they can produce the education that touches and teaches, and which allows us to acquire the necessary knowledge to solve society's problems.

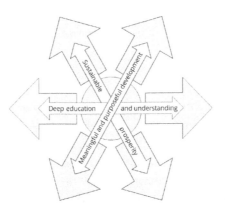

Figure 8: Bildung Rose collaboration

When we are prepared to reach across the Rose and collaborate, particularly with the domain furthest away, power can be distributed across society, and we can have freedom and responsibility in all domains. By doing so, power becomes more complex by decentralization, and when decision-makers in all domains serve freedom, responsibility, and society as a whole through their domain, the inhabitants can enjoy sustainable prosperity, deep understanding, meaning, and a sense of purpose in the overall development. In short: enlightenment, empowerment, and emancipation; bildung. When we as individuals pursue knowledge in all domains and when the political power sustains, actively supports and promotes all domains plus collaboration among them, then we can have stable societies and non-corrupt institutions.

It is therefore crucial that decision-makers in all domains and from the top to the bottom of every organization care about society as a whole and value being a team player on behalf of society and reach across the Rose, and it is crucial that we all have the bildung to do so.

Just like folk-bildung 1.0 at the folk-high-schools promoted all domains, so did folk-bildung 2.0, Cultural Radicalism. Cultural Radicalism was universal values (ethics) tured into industrial design (aesthetics, production, technology), poetry and theatrical plays (aesthetics) and satire (aesthetics and politics), and a political ideology (power), and it found itself in a constant struggle with religion and old moral values (narrative).

Pushbacks

The one overall phenomenon that leads to an increase in mental complexity is when we realize that our existing assumptions about the world were insufficient or wrong. The "Jeez, what an idiot I have been!" As long as our assumptions, our mental model of the world, our worldview, or epistemology is confirmed, there is no need to change or expand; we may expand our knowledge, but we do not grow much. But when we have to reconfigure our model, our world view to match reality, we grow. Especially, if we have to revise several assumptions simultaneously and the pain causes us to thoroughly deal with ourselves, and why we held a wrong or too simplistic assumption; i.e., when we have to tear out the pipes and redo the plumbing in part of our mental mansion, then we grow.

Piaget called it accommodation of schemata, schemata being our mental models of the world. A more everyday-word would be an "offense," something that shakes us without doing real harm. Instead, it makes us stronger. As the American author Greg Lukianoff (b. 1974) and psychologist Jonathan Haidt (b. 1963) term it: we are anti-fragile. We need pushbacks to become robust or resilient and to grow.

Piaget said that along with children's physical development, a child's mind evolves through an on-going process of *assimilation* and *accommodation* of *schemata*, i.e. mental models of the world. When a child encounters a new event that is consistent with an existing schema or mental model of the world, the schema is confirmed and there is assimilation. But when a child encounters a new event that is not consistent with an existing schema, when something unexpected occurs, the child must either modify this existing model of the world or form an entirely new one, which means growth.

Interestingly enough, Hume already knew this regarding young adults:

> There is no man so young and unexperienced, as not to have formed, from observation, many general and just maxims concerning human affairs and the conduct of life, but it must be confessed, that, when a man comes to put these in practice, he will be extremely liable to error, till time and farther experience both enlarge these maxims, and teach him their proper use and application.

Kant's *Kritik der reinen Vernunft / Critique of Pure Reason* looked at it differently. Kant conceptualized some organizing structures of our meaning-making that were given *a priori,* i.e., these structures have no inherent content, and they cannot suffer pushbacks. But once Kant's philosophy had 'opened the mind,' so to speak, to philosophical inquiry, others explored how we, over the course of our life, can change that mind.

Fichte, who was also in Jena in the 1790s, was the first philosopher to explore how and through what process the human spirit (or mind) and the spirit of the world co-evolve; he was the first to develop a so-called Ideal system. According to Fichte's Ideal system, the self is only an absolute "I" when it becomes self-aware, and this can only happen when it has to react to the unexpected; the self becomes autonomous because it reacts to pushbacks. If there was no pushback, no friction, the self would be one with its activities and fully absorbed in them. In order to develop self-awareness, the individual must thus allow pushbacks and ensure that there are "bones of contention."

Hegel, also in Jena, came after Fichte and wrote:

Bildung, therefore, is, in its absolute determination, the liberation and the labor towards the higher liberation, namely, the absolute point of transition into the infinitely subjective substantiality of morality, which is no longer immediate, natural, but spiritual.

Bildung is, according to those old German Idealists, an inevitable process towards a freedom that is no longer spontaneous and natural but moral and spiritual. This spirit is in society and in the individual: the world moves towards higher ethical standards, and so do individuals. According to Hegel, the process is dialectical, which means that the world changes by facing its own inner obstacles, pushbacks, and overcoming them. As do people.

Both Grundtvig and Kold read Fichte, and definitely, Grundtvig also read both Hume, Kant, and Hegel. The folk-high-schools were conceived based on some major intellectual pushbacks.

What bildung and lack of bildung look like

Societies differ, families and circumstances differ, and yet, in order to live a fulfilling life and be a good friend, spouse, citizen, and colleague, there are milestones to be aware of:

- By age 4, impulses should generally be under control, but emotions may still be overwhelming.
- By age 5, one should have friends and be able to play in groups.
- By age 10, one should be able to play by collective rules, such as in sports; one should be able to be a team player when the rules are explicit.
- By age 15, one should be able to be a team player in a 'tribe' and be loyal to that tribe, even when nobody is watching. The 'tribe' may be a workplace or a gang, same thing.

Friends, employers, colleagues, teammates, sexual partners etc. expect that one understands the rules, also when they are not explicit and/or constantly expressed, and that one can be trusted.

- By age 18, one should be able to be a team player in society and care about one's greater society, its norms and rules. That is why we allow 18-year-olds to vote, and why young men (and in some places women) can join the army or be conscripted. One should also increasingly be able to put one's own short-term needs aside for the long-term benefits of significant others, i.e., children and spouse.
- By age 25, all of the above should be second nature.
- By age 40, questioning the expectations of others and the norms of society is about time.
- By age 70, others should ask for one's advice; if that is not the case, something went wrong.

Some may be slower, some quicker. Girls are usually faster than boys (even Rousseau mentioned that). One should not despair if some are a bit slow, most will catch up. This development should be a goal, though, a rule of thumb, and we can scaffold it through care, upbringing, culture, education, and giving each other the necessary pushbacks and freedom to make mistakes; nobody will learn and grow without mistakes.

In Danish, we have a unique word: *fremelske*, which literally means: to bring forth with love. There is probably nothing greater than to *fremelske*, to bring forth with love, the best and noblest in others, and to bring forth with love is really the only thing that works regarding the development listed above. The with-love-forth-bringing may, of course, happen as care, conversations, education, giving of advice, teaching by example, and even rebuke, just sitting around and forth-loving no matter how intense it might be is not enough, one also has to unfold this love. But the point is: forced love is not love; one cannot bring-forth-with-love without actually loving and caring about the person. Which is why loving and caring teachers who enter into a personal relationship with their pupils are the ones that make a difference.

What is crucial to understand about our development is that from any one of the later phases in life, one can understand the previous phases, but one cannot from an earlier phase in life understand what it is like to live with the experience, perspective, and maturity of the later phases. They need to be brought forth with love and evolve first. This also goes for Kegan's five stages or layers:

- **As self-consolidating**, one cannot grasp what it is like to be self-governing. One cannot grasp what it is like to think of the expectations and emotions of others before one satisfies one's own needs.
- **As self-governing**, one cannot grasp what it is like to be self-authoring. One cannot grasp what it is like to mentally step outside the collective Us, see it as an object, dissect it, be critical of it, and perhaps even appreciate when outsiders criticize it. As self-governing, one organizes the world according to 'Us versus Them,' and the younger one is, and the newer one is to self-governing, the more black-and-white, either-or one's view of 'Us versus Them' tends to be; more fanatic, less tolerant.
- **As self-authoring**, one cannot grasp what it is like to be self-transforming. One cannot grasp what it is like to get more pleasure out of seeing others grow than to grow oneself.

Tolerance tends to emerge with self-authoring; pursuing one's own, true, individual path in life also makes us realize that in order for me to divert from the norm, others must have the same right to stray too. Appreciation of diversity tends to emerge with self-transforming, when we enjoy seeing personal, truly individual growth in others. Appreciating Loke as well as Thor does not come easy!

The tricky behavior that looks like ego-development

There are at least two kinds of behavior that look like something they may not be. Before I go into describing them, some words of caution: the way Kegan describes ego-development, there is a progression in emotional development and mental complexity, and his model is generally understood as 'once you reach a certain stage of development, your entire being has transformed.' That has a lot of merit to it, and we do go through fundamental changes in our emotional mode of being throughout life. That said, by combining Kegan's ego-development with the Circles of Belonging, I have also showed how education and life experience define what kind of emotional and cognitive involvement we are capable of in different contexts. Ego-development is not as clear-cut as it may appear, which is why I prefer bildung: its complexity and elusiveness allows for human variation, different circumstances, and quirks of personality.

Tricky behavior 1: self-consolidation or self-authoring?

Since both self-consolidation and self-authoring are about living out and expressing that which is uniquely one's true emotions and self, it can be hard to figure out if your charming new colleague, boss, romantic date, friend etc., is self-consolidating or self-authoring. The difference is whether:

- The person has remained more or less self-consolidating since childhood and never went through the self-governing phase, or if
- the person actually did become a team player in their youth, evolved beyond it, and found his/her true self and the courage to step outside the norms and pursue his/her true self.

The first person is not capable of subjugating him/herself to collective interest and to 'take one for the team;' the second person is the one you want in your life.

In many social contexts in postmodern society, not being a team player is no problem for success. The highly intelligent kid who can out-smart parents and teachers and nails every test and exam, may grow up to become a highly successful professor or CEO with no social con-science. A similar path may unfold for the rich kid who never faced any pushbacks and never realizes that a sense of entitlement and other peo-ple's sucking up to money is blocking his/her view, and (s)he is, in effect, still behaving like a 10-year-old.

Figuring out whether you are dealing with an adult self-consolidator or a self-authoring adult can be hard.

Tricky behavior 2: self-governing or self-authoring?

Part of maturing beyond self-governing is an emerging tolerance of people who deviate from the norm; with self-authoring, one tends to become increasingly tolerant, and as self-transforming, one even appre-ciates the difference and the pushbacks that come from different per-spectives on life.

Tolerance is a hallmark value and norm of modernity: we can only have liberal democracy and open societies if the leading culture accepts differences of opinion, lifestyle, race, sexual orientation, religion, etc. Free-dom for Loke as well as for Thor; only Schiller's Moral Person can look beyond the emotions and the conformity and handle political freedom.

Exposing hidden power structures is a hallmark of postmodernism; the tolerance claimed by modernity had blind spots: there is still struc-tural racism and sexism, still binary gender norms that define language and culture, and still social injustice, which favors some and not others. Though there are fewer privileges than ever before, there are still privi-leges around.

So, what happens when postmodern deconstruction of the modern "tolerance" is taught to youth that are new to self-governing? When tol-erance and deconstruction of existing power structures are taught as a norm to an age group that tends to see the world as either-or black-and-white Us-versus-Them?

A quick look at college campuses, particularly in the US and Canada, reveals fanatic identity politics. Swathes of Western youth have been socialized into tolerant norms (nothing wrong with that) but without the emotional maturity to actually *be* tolerant. One can be promoting tolerant norms intolerantly.

Developmental psychology can help us make this analysis, but bildung is the toolbox that may offer a way out of it.

Part of postmodernism is the deconstruction of the historical narrative as a progression of the human experience; in postmodern school systems, history is taught as snapshots in time, and within each snapshot, the power structures are exposed. Postmodernism tends to dismiss a linear understanding of history altogether: History does not come with a purpose or direction; progress and setbacks mingle, and history unfolds in often chaotic ways. From an academic perspective, the postmodern approach to history is crucial; we could not be civilized civilizations in a globalized world without it. But the fact that history does not have a purpose is not the same as there being no timelines in history: some things happened before other things, and the later things could not have happened without the earlier ones. Therefore, the postmodern deconstruction of history may not be the best way to teach history to children, teenagers, and young adults who are in the process of figuring out where they belong in the world. If we teach them where they belong in a power hierarchy and not the process that brought us to where we are, we should not expect an ability to relate to much more than the power structures their schools have shown them. The result is a generation of young people with no sense of history, who see only power structures and who preach tolerance without being able to practice it. Part of the bildung needed is thus both better teaching of history as developments that are unfolding and an understanding of what people were struggling with as history unfolded. Mr. Schimmelmann did not want to give up his slaves, but he found the conditions under the transatlantic slave transportations so abhorrent they had to stop, and he had the political power to do it. At least the Danish part of it. He eventually did. But he made sure enough Africans could be shipped to St. Thomas before the ban so that they could keep reproducing. History and circumstances are messy, and so are people.

We all need the ability to be able to identify with people under different circumstances, both historically and right now, and we need to be moral people who can stand up to moral wrongs. Hence, we need both history as a connected narrative, postmodern deconstruction and bildung. According to the ILO and Walk Free Foundation, there are currently an estimated 40,000,000 people living in slavery, 71 % of them women, 25 % of them children, and the issue is barely on the political agenda. We do not seem to mind being "Schimmelmanns" ourselves.

A bildung Toolbox

As we are facing more complex challenges as individuals, as societies and as a species, we need all the bildung we can get, and we need it to be as hands-on as possible without turning it into more standardized, spreadsheet-ready, measurable education. We, therefore, need some sort of bildung toolbox, hence the above models. This 'toolbox' is not enough, of course; we also need to develop the appropriate teaching methods for this.

In different countries, freedom and responsibility are distributed differently, because of politics, but also because of different levels in formal education and bildung. Most governments still do not trust and provide sufficient education for the population, and school systems are still set up to produce self-governing adults who would never dare think for themselves or question anything, least of all the political leadership.

Food for thought
Did anything in this chapter rub you the wrong way?
What?

A FUTURE OF BILDUNG

Suggestions and a bigger perspective

This final chapter contains some of my personal suggestions as to how we can move on. As a species, we need education and bildung that matches the complexities of the 21st century. We need metamodern education and bildung. We also need responsibility in all Circles of Belonging and in all seven domains of the Bildung Rose throughout those circles. We need folk-bildung 3.0. How can we do that?

If there is anything good coming out of the COVID-19 pandemic, as it looks from a spring 2020 perspective, it is the radical action from governments in putting people's lives and medical care above the market. Faced with an obvious existential crisis, we do have our priorities straight. Now we just need the bildung to keep putting humanity and the wellbeing of our planet first.

As a species, we are at a crossroads, and these are, as I see it, the two paths we can choose between:

A. We **do not** make a conscious choice about what kind of future we want, technological development continues according to market interests, and climate change and extinction of species get beyond our control. We install constant surveillance with facial recognition to monitor everybody, and we let AI make a host of our decisions. Since AI has no actual human experience such as embodiment, embeddedness or spirit, and it bases its decisions on historical data, it is most likely going to fight new ideas and self-authoring while it rewards self-governing. Civilization will grind to a halt, and everybody will conform to AI and historical data.

B. We **do** make a conscious choice that we do not want to become slaves of our own inventions, and we prioritize life on the planet above the market; we promote freedom and responsibility, autonomy and integration, meaning-making and spirit, i.e., bildung.

If we choose option A, the life of future generations is almost impossible to imagine. If we choose option B, future generations may enjoy the same levels of freedom, security, meaning, purpose, fun, and prosperity that we do in Denmark, Finland, Iceland, Norway, and Sweden today, and as a species, we may be able to make it even better than that. Unfortunately, option A is the 'easy' choice because we do not have to make hard decisions right now; that scenario is on track to unfold. Option B requires that we change many current priorities and put humans, nature, ethics, and the development of a different economic model that is long-term sustainable before everything else. Speaking against option B are, among other things, that the debt and investments that have already been made need to be amortized. As a species, we are caught in our economy like a fly in a spider's web, and we do not know how to escape the web.

What does bildung feel like?

Bildung can be horrible and it can be fun. Bildung and ego-development can come from making horrible mistakes, the *faux pas* that 'teaches you a lesson!' At the societal level, COVID-19 will no doubt be such a lesson. But bildung can also come from facing the right kinds of challenges at the right time, in the right place, with the right people, and be very meaningful in an encouraging way. It can be fun. Pushbacks can be harsh, and pushbacks can make us laugh.

Compared to developmental psychology, bildung has, given its educational and aesthetic components, the added aspect that one can expose oneself to it in so many ways, and one can begin any time. If one does not want to go out and have one's worldview challenged among other people, one can begin at home, the only thing needed is curiosity.

Concretely, you can listen to some music that seems strange and try to get the story behind it in order to 'open' it; have somebody who is enthusiastic about it explain why it is great! Do the same with a painting or any other piece of art that does not make sense yet; the reason somebody made it was because they needed to say something that could not be said in any other way. What is it they are trying to say? You don't have to agree with them.

Or grab a novel, preferably one of the classics that has stood the test of time, make a cup of coffee, find your favorite armchair, and read yourself into another person's mind. And then, by identifying with that character, explore the world from that person's point of view as you read and consider: What choices would I have made in that same situation? Would I have stood the moral test? The ethical test?

The Danish philosopher Søren Kierkegaard (1813-1855) read plenty of Schiller and explored aesthetic and ethical aspects of life in his own writings. With a great sense of humor and satirical whit, Kierkegaard described such characters as the Petit Bourgeois (self-governing), the Aesthetic (the transition between self-governing and self-authoring, i.e., Kegan 3½), and the Ethic (self-authoring). Then he made an interesting analysis of the two kinds of heroes we generally meet in literature: The aesthetic hero struggles against something outside himself; the Ethic hero struggles against something inside himself.

When picking a novel to go on a bildung journey in your armchair, pick one with an Ethic hero. Usually, that is what you find in the classics; when literature is at its best, the hero fights both outside and inside himself. If you start fighting with him or her, that is bildung.

Metamodern education and bildung

The postmodern world with its deconstruction of almost everything and constant relativizing, has prevented a lot of honest, deep emotional connection to cultural heritage and other people. There is always this "distance." It has left many morally alone, as Fromm called it; we are massively in an existential vacuum, and it feels horrible. The corona lockdown has not made the situation any better. We, therefore, need something else.

So far, the education and bildung we have offered children, youth, and each other as adults through history have been either:

- **Indigenous**: oral narratives and collective rituals telling how humans are a part of nature and the spiritual world and through that, how to survive and thrive in a small tribe, or:
- **Premodern**: top-down dissemination of moral and religious written, codified Truths, often authoritarian, but also with a deep emotional timbre and amazing aesthetics; grand narratives that deal with tough moral and ethical dilemmas; traditions that teach how to survive, thrive and keep together in societies of hundreds of thousands of strangers of the same faith, i.e., an imagined community, or:
- **Modern**: industrialized top-down dissemination of scientific facts and rationality; the technical, productivity and skill-enhancing knowledge that allows a person to survive and thrive in a modern economy and nation-states of millions of strangers; the education only rarely encouraging people to ask questions, or:
- **Postmodern**: deconstruction of narratives, rituals, truth, science, and rationality; political correctness that allows a person to encounter people from everywhere without offending anybody, and as a consequence: there is not that much to hold onto that could make life meaningful and allow the individual to thrive and thus survive.

Each of the four kinds of education and bildung has their own qualities: the earlier the form, the better it matches the learning style of our Stone Age brain; the later the form, the better it matches the complexity of the late 20th century.

This is the 21st century, and we need metamodern education and bildung that offer all of the above.

Metamodern formal education

Formal education, including age-appropriate bildung is the minimum education that any state should guarantee everybody, i.e., that which citizens must be willing to grant each other if there is to be a functioning society where any healthy adult can support themselves and contribute and thrive as a citizen. A society that does not provide free access to the knowledge and skills that enable people to survive and live in dignity by their own effort should be considered a failed society, a failed state—and a society that does not also provide bildung will fail as a state.

Metamodern pre-, primary and secondary education

One path to pursue in order to educate our Stone Age minds so that we can thrive in the 21st century is to revisit Herder. Not in order to see peoples of past or present as matching some level of bildung, but to match our educational systems and their curricula to our emotional development.

Since we are still born as hunter-gatherers, let toddlers begin their bildung journey in nature, in the Stone Age, so to speak. Let them play, explore nature, get some great stories from indigenous mythologies, and learn to keep a rhythm, dance, and sing in pre-school and kindergarten. Add horticulture, tool making, farming, and cooking around age 5.

Around age 6, children should be ready for the Bronze Age. The production, technologies, sciences, narratives, aesthetics, and not least the writing systems and symbolic worlds of the great civilizations of that era should capture their imagination.

Telling indigenous and Bronze Age mythologies in kindergarten would expand the vocabularies and imagination of the children, and connect them to our shared world heritage.

The Iron Age includes the invention of the alphabet, the Axial Age with the emergence of the major world religions, and discoveries, technologies, narratives, aesthetics, architecture, and wisdoms with meaning-making potential from around age 7, and with plenty of material to teach until around age 9.

Until around 1400 CE, two of the cultural codes emerged around the globe: prehistoric indigenous culture and premodern culture; then Europe embarked on a cultural journey that differed fundamentally from the rest of the world. Gutenberg's printing press from around 1440 allowed an exchange of thoughts and ideas that did not happen anywhere else. Combined with capitalism and colonialism, the increased flow of resources and ideas produced 500 years of development in the West that is unparalleled. Beginning in the Renaissance, all seven domains of Western societies transformed radically and gained mutual autonomy, and the West took the lead regarding modernity: freedom of speech, freedom of religion, individual rights, and equal rights for all.

On the one hand, it is Eurocentric to suggest that school children between age 10 and 15 around the globe should learn what went on in Europe and the US in all seven domains of the Bildung Rose during the 500 years between Gutenberg and the UN. On the other hand, the European Renaissance, Enlightenment, colonialism, Romanticism, and overall modernity define the globe today. Modern medicine, science, industrialization, political institutions, conflicts, pollution, the fossil economy, the environmental crises, global media, social media, and the way capitalism and colonialism have defined that development, can only be understood, and, therefore, can only be handled properly, when one understands the historical development across all seven domains in the West from around 1440 until 1948. While teaching this, there are plenty of opportunities to also teach how that development affected the rest of the world, including how Westerners stole both human lives and natural resources just about everywhere and destroyed other societies and civilizations.

The development during the Renaissance, in many intricate ways, matches the capacities of the mind of the 10-year-old. The new technological inventions of the period were mechanical and would be great fun for 10-year-olds to recreate. An almost eerie correlation between the Renaissance and the 10-year-old, self-consolidating mind is that psychologists often refer to the age group of 10-year-olds as having a Machiavellian mind. Who knows, maybe reading some of Niccolò Machiavelli's (1469-1527) *The Prince* might actually make a lot of sense to 10-year-olds?

The Enlightenment was the age of the steam engine, mechanics, Mozart, human rights, the transatlantic slave trade, slavery, and the American and French Revolutions, and the period would be the perfect challenge for 11-12-year-olds. The emotional development of 13-year-olds makes them ready for Romanticism, nationalism, and democracy plus Beethoven, modern science, Darwin, electricity, the British Empire, and the literature and social commentary of Victor Hugo (1802-1885) and Charles Dickens (1812-1870). From age 14, learning about the production, technology, science, ethics, narratives, aesthetics, and politics of modernity would match their cognitive maturity.

Around 16, they should be ripe for postmodernism, quantum physics, and systems thinking, and if they have the above mentioned knowledge, they also have enough knowledge to start deconstructing and relativizing.

With a curriculum like that, the development of the seven domains of society would be connected through time and in relation to global development, and since barely any spot on Earth went unexplored and unexploited by the Europeans, the historical development also relates to the children's own country. It would also explain the position of their country in the global economy.

Everybody should, of course, learn about the history of their own country and its political relations to its neighbors. It was not only the Europeans who fought countless wars, enslaved others, created wonderful art, and invented new things.

Combining all domains of the Rose with historical development, their inner world of the mind would be able to relate to all aspects of the outer world and why things are the way they are. Everybody would get a sense of history, of their place in time, in culture and in nature; everybody would be able to relate to cultures and civilizations around the globe, and to the world heritage of indigenous, pre-modern, modern, and postmodern cultures. Everybody would have experienced how societal domains are interconnected and co-evolve over time. With knowledge about all domains, everybody would have the prerequisite knowledge to pursue a meaningful life and with specialization in tertiary education; they would know enough to decide what would be most meaningful to them. With such knowledge, we could develop a metamodern culture with both a global outlook and deep local cultural roots everywhere.

Throughout both primary and secondary education, teachers should have resources, time, and freedom to do what they are trained to do: take responsibility for giving each child the challenges that give them the right amounts of both ease, excitement, joy, and pushbacks in order for them to grow. To bring forth with love, the best in each child. This is, in fact, what well-educated pedagogues and teachers know how to do.

With robots taking over much of the production of physical goods and AI taking over a number of academic jobs, employing more pedagogues and teachers and letting them have the time and resources to actually educate and support the emotional development of the children should be a no-brainer. Why else would we let technology take over millions of people's jobs and livelihoods if not in order for us to work with that which really matters and to make life richer and more meaningful? And what could be more meaningful than being a teacher with sufficient resources and freedom to teach and see each child flourish and grow?

Tertiary Education

We need experts with deep knowledge in their field, and that of course requires focus on one topic, but we also need experts who can collaborate across several, if not all domains of society. There are two paths to pursue here; one is making sure that besides the specialized field, every tertiary education also teaches the broader societal context and the basics of all domains. The second is that everybody should get at least two tertiary educations, preferably from different domains. A third option, of course, is that everybody does both.

By acquiring more than one professional expertise, one gets more than one perspective on the world, more than one professional epistemology. It is like the double consciousness of culture: with more than one perspective, one can acquire depth of perception. One can look at the analysis and patterns of thought from one discipline through the epistemology of the other discipline. In an increasingly complex world, we need experts who can do that; we need people who are experts in more than one field who can analyze, think, produce new hypotheses, be creative, and see new potentials by combining two or more sets of knowledge.

De Bildung Academie

It is also possible to do what some university students and a professor did in Amsterdam, the Netherlands: In 2014, they realized that something was missing from their education and they created *De Bildung Academie*. It started as an add-on to their formal education, a separate five month program for people who had completed their bachelor's degree and who were still studying or who had completed their master's degree within the past two years. As of 2020, they are now transforming educations around the Netherlands and are spreading into the rest of Europe with their program. Part of their approach at the universities is this:

> The only thing needed to create Bildung programs in higher education is to let go of the conviction that you have something to teach. Education needs to focus on exploring questions rather than providing answers.

That is probably very close to what Grundtvig experienced in the UK and Kold provided in his school.

Folk-bildung 3.0

Smart populations grant each other folk-bildung, not just formal education; smart individuals are willing to pay for being surrounded by people of education and bildung beyond what is necessary for survival. These smart people are also willing to volunteer as coaches, teachers, scout leaders, etc. and to pay for more bildung for themselves and their children.

Folk-bildung for children

Modern societies already have folk-bildung for children, but to adults, it tends to look like leisure and fun. The point is: it is both leisure, fun, and crucially, bildung:

Team sports teach children to be team players and to play by rules not defined by themselves. If we do not learn this between ages 6 and 10 when conforming is a challenge, and it makes us proud when we succeed, it is very hard to enjoy this kind of subjugation later. Anybody who has had a spouse, boss, or colleagues with no team player skills knows how horrible one's life becomes around such people. If we are the ones without the team player skills, we are not necessarily likely to realize that we are constantly being self-consolidating and a pain to be around.

Playing an instrument or singing in a choir teaches children to listen and to listen in. Besides the fact that being able to play an instrument is cool, that playing music allows us to express emotions in a different way, and that playing and singing feels great, learning to play teaches motor skills, focus, concentration, and a host of other skills that are very useful throughout life.

Dancing and folk dancing teaches cultural heritage, listening, coordination, motor skills, following the correct steps, moves, patterns and routines; typically, they are also communal. See, bildung can be fun!

Scouts teach children to take responsibility and to circulate responsibility and leadership in small groups, called patrols. They also teach practical skills and diverse kinds of knowledge; they teach it as a group endeavor and reward everybody with a badge to put on their uniform. To many liberal adults, the mere thought of putting children in uniform is appalling, but at age 7 to 12 and even into their teens, living up to the honor code of a uniform is a cognitive achievement and earning the badges are a source of great pride. The scouts teach children to be good peers, to take care of everybody in the group, to take responsibility, and to show agency, initiative, and leadership.

Doing **amateur theater** and playing **roleplaying games** allows, among other things, for playing around with roles and identities.

Finally, having a **vegetable garden**, be it through **4H** or just a patch of soil somewhere, teaches planning, patience, connection to nature, and where food comes from.

I think we tend to overlook how important these after school and weekend activities are for children and for society, and how crucial it is that there are teens, young adults and adults who volunteer to make these bildung activities available and affordable to all children. Unfortunately, they are still too expensive for many children and their families, and it requires adults who take responsibility for it and have the skills to do it. Luckily, it is usually deeply meaningful to volunteer. An added bonus from the volunteering adults is the different kind of relationship that can emerge between volunteers and children: the adults are not paid to be there and they are not family, they only do it because they care.

Folk-bildung for teens and young adults

Both team sports and the scouts are perfect places for young adults to volunteer as leaders. By doing so, one takes responsibility for others and for an organization, and one gets to teach others how to play fair and according to shared rules. Volunteering as a sports coach or scout leader is also a great way to get some pushback in one's teen years and early adulthood.

Besides this, postmodern societies have very little to offer young adults with regards to moral values and learning how to take responsibility outside Family 1 and personal peer-groups. Youth chapters of political parties are a great way to start exploring politics and civic duties and to get some pushbacks too, but if one does not identify with an existing party, that may be a problem. We need to come up with more youth bildung that can challenge and inspire teens and young adults.

The after-schools in Denmark and the folk-high-schools in all of the Nordic countries still work wonders for the age groups 14-18 and 18-25. The world just needs more of them, and they need to re-introduce history and narratives, plus the latest science and technology as part of their curricula. There are 260 after-schools in Denmark and some 26,000 kids out of an annual cohort of around 60,000 attend. There are 73 folk-high-schools in Denmark today, with a total of some 11,000 students per year.

But we also need something for those who cannot go to a folk-high-school for five months or an after-school for a year.

One of the most obvious places to promote bildung among 15 to 25-year-olds is to improve the education they are getting anyway. Their main obligation at that age is to study; the main obligation of the education system ought to be that it is a bildung system as well as an educational system. The many hours teens and young adults spend learning should not merely turn them into members of the workforce, it should cover the full Rose, and it should challenge them to become good team players and autonomous persons. It should give them pushbacks and let them struggle with moral and ethical dilemmas so that they can feel themselves and learn to think for themselves. What De Bildung Academie started at the university in Amsterdam ought to be standard at all universities.

Scouts+

It is important, though, that we not only broaden our mind and meet others during school and work hours; part of a functioning democracy is that the citizens meet and bond outside family, peer groups and work, that we contribute to a strong social fabric in our local community.

One suggestion for providing young adults with some meaningful challenges could be some sort of **Civic Scouts**, providing age-appropriate challenges through all seven domains of the bildung Rose. Experienced seniors ought to volunteer as leaders, mentors, and teachers here, and the young people ought to be mature enough to do most of the organizing themselves if there is a well-defined framework for it. These are just suggestions for activities in all domains:

- **Production**: this could tap into the maker, prepper and DIY culture that is already emerging, but it could also be wine tasting, coffee, and tea connoisseuring, gourmet cooking, vegetable gardening, making and repairing clothes, proper housekeeping and cleaning, household economics, upcycling trash, and surviving in the forest for a few days equipped with a tent and a Swiss army knife.
- **Technology**: setting up a website, understanding algorithms and basic programming, repairing a bicycle, driving, backing and parking a truck with a trailer, learning how to handle and fight a fire, building a windmill, and setting up a house for being off-grid.
- **Science**: first aid, acquiring conversational level in at least two sciences, and completing an experiment in one of them following the scientific method and ethics.
- **Ethics**: discussing production, technology, and science from an ethical perspective, studying and discussing the philosophical classics on ethics, and learning how to facilitate a discussion and a study circle.
- **Narrative**: knowing world history, the major religions of the world, and a handful of literary classics.
- **Aesthetics**: learning calligraphy, drawing and painting, studying indigenous art from around the globe, the art forms of the empires and religions through history, and the –isms of modern art, and creating one's own art and design.
- **Power**: learning a martial art, studying the history of war (and peace), such as The Art of War by Sun Tzu (544-496), or the classical texts by Plato, Machiavelli, and Hugo Grotius (1583-1645), the constitution of one's country, and the

major political declarations of independence and human rights. Study the programs of the political parties and deconstruct them.

As much as possible based on curiosity and asking questions; the angles on each activity can thereby be more masculine or feminine as people please.

It would, by the way, be the perfect setting for finding that particular other: rather than basing one's romantic interests on who is the best dancer after half a bottle of vodka, one could increasingly focus on not just whom one would like to sleep with, but also whom one would like to wake up with.

Folk-bildung for adults

Today, there is a plethora of adult education available, not just in the Nordics, but across the West. Unfortunately, the majority of schools and programs focus on upgrading people's professional skills, or they are evening classes for personal hobbies—which are important, but the democratic, transformative, empowering, emancipatory, and civic aspects of adult education have more or less vanished. The bildung part, the pushbacks, the deep conversations that challenge our worldviews, the democratic training, the folk-bildung that expands our Circles of Belonging from the nationalism we grew up with to continental and global consciousness and conscience are missing.

What is missing is also the latest knowledge within all seven domains of the Bildung Rose, and adult folk-bildung ought to provide it:

- **Production**: What are the conditions and consequences of production and consumption in the 21st century?
- **Technology**: What is the cutting edge of technology?
- **Science**: What is the cutting edge of knowledge?
- **Ethics**: What should be our ethical principles facing current changes and challenges?

- **Narrative**: What are the narratives that hold our societies, our communities, and our lives together?
- **Aesthetics**: What challenges our epistemology and provides pushbacks?
- **Power**: Who is in power where, by what means, and how do we as citizens secure the future of democracy?

  Plus: How can each domain contribute to protecting the environment and all circles of belonging?

Dealing with this together with other adults is crucial if we are to make sound decisions in our own lives and collectively. It is particularly crucial that people in power have these conversations, and we need moderators for such conversations.

Retrofitting local communities and shopping malls

As these lines are written, online classes are the new black, and distance socializing keeps everybody 6 ft. apart, but that won't last forever. So why not dream big? A civilization of bildung, where the richness of our inner world enjoys the same attention as our bodies do in fitness centers? Where we go shopping for knowledge with the family during the weekends the same way we take the family to the shopping mall? Where we enjoy luxurious bildung retreats the way old-fashioned elites enjoy spas, skiing, and 'after skiing' in the bar? Mental spa, bildung and 'after bildung' in the bar?

How come shopping malls have marble floors, and our schools are run down? How come, it is normal to organize drinking parties, dinner parties, and barbecues, but not thinking parties, learning parties, and campfire wisdom chats? How come, cultural salons have become popular in academic circles in parts of Europe, but mostly for highbrow entertainment, not in order to change anything?

Why do the vast majority of adults around the globe not demand access to the latest knowledge and the ability to grasp the development and the world in which they struggle to make ends meet? Why do we not empower ourselves and each other with the knowledge necessary to develop societies where everybody thrives?

In the aftermath of the corona lockdown, there will be different travel and trade patterns. Why not retrofit shopping malls and hotels to become bildung venues? Rather than venues for the exchange of money and physical goods, make them venues for exchanges of questions, thoughts, ideas, knowledge, art, music, conversations, stories – and money. Why sit passively around watching movies about others who live life when you could be living yourself, in a movie theater full of singing people where you could sing along?

Even before the lockdown, as local communities lost their local commerce to internet trade, there were plenty of empty stores and even entire shopping malls that could be turned into folk-bildung venues. Instead of shopping temples, folk-bildung temples with the best of contemporary art and on-site affordable quality cooking. Instead of sitting at home in front of our screens and ordering stuff most of us really do not need and which is bad for the environment anyway, we could go out and eat, drink and study with others.

Why wait for somebody else to take the initiative? Why not do as the Danish farmers, pastors, teachers, philanthropists, and concerned citizens of 175 years ago did, and transform our societies? From the bottom, with the resources available locally and out of our own initiative? What is holding us back?

The best investment is in people

Universal, public primary, and secondary education are considered a necessity in most, if not all modern societies. But that's it. Tertiary education is optional and is generally considered a benefit for the individual, whether it is paid for by the individual or by the government. For some strange reason, in the national accounting, education is considered an expense for society, not an investment.

The reason this is strange, is that society as a whole becomes richer, more stable and more democratic the better and the more educated the population is and the more bildung everybody has. Education and bildung are public goods that benefit all; we are all better off if we are surrounded by well-educated people of emotional and moral maturity. With bildung (not necessarily with more education, but with more bildung), people see the bigger picture and take responsibility; they don't just think in a short-sighted manner, and about what would benefit themselves.

Imagine two different communities or nation states:

- **The first community or nation state:**
  - The majority of 16-year-olds take responsibility for their peer-groups and are loyal team-players on behalf of society, they enjoy the trust of both peers and adults, and they have a sense of what might be a worthwhile education and job for them.
    - They are self-governing regarding Circles of Belonging 1-6, conscious about Circles 7-10, and have a basic insight into all seven domains of the Rose.
    - During a pandemic, they feel a moral obligation to protect the vulnerable and disadvantaged.
  - The majority of people above the age of 30 are responsible, self-motivated adults who can take the perspective of others, they care about their country, have a global outlook and insist on human rights and dignity and protecting nature whatever they do. They also have the moral courage to stand up to authority and, say, alert their boss if (s)he is making a mistake. They consider how they can best use their personal potential and get some pushbacks and new challenges.
    - They are self-authoring, conscious about all 10 Circles of Belonging, enjoying a sense of responsi-

bility and initiative in Circles 1-6, consider the well-being of Circles 7-10, and are well-versed in one or two domains with broad knowledge of all seven.

- During a pandemic, they follow the guidelines impeccably and keep holding authorities accountable. They insist that the guidelines make sense, and if they don't they keep asking until the authorities have their act together.

• The majority of 50+ adults, particularly people in leadership positions are capable of seeing other people's perspectives and needs, can help others grow, see the social dynamics between individuals and groups, and can promote collaboration among people; they consider the wellbeing of both individuals, groups and the planet as a whole.

- They are self-transforming, feel responsible towards all 10 Circles of Belonging, have expert knowledge in one or two domains of the Rose plus a relatively deep understanding of the rest, and are capable of combining knowledge from different domains.
- During a pandemic, they have the moral authority and wisdom to make complying with the pandemic protective measures meaningful to the young and silly.

• **The second community or nation-state:**

  • The majority of 16-year-olds can only relate to their family 1 and peer-group, and they generally approach the world based on the question "What's in it for me?"

    - They are self-consolidating, have a sense of responsibility towards Circles of Belonging 1-3, some consciousness regarding Circles 5 and 6 and no real understanding of any of the seven domains, how each domain contributes to society or what would be the point in working in any of them except making a living.

- Sneezing into their sleeve seems overwhelming.

- The majority of 30-year-olds are team-players on behalf of family, community and nation and/or religion, mostly out of fears about what others might think if they weren't.
    - They are self-governing and conscious about Circles 1-6, but they are mostly concerned with what others might think, and they have a limited understanding of the seven domains.
    - During a pandemic curfew, they are not trusted by their government.

- A minority of adults above the age of 50 dare take personal responsibility and speak up against formal authority and/or tradition. They strongly believe in their nation and/or religion, they are conscious about the rest of the world but do not think it concerns them, and they are experienced but not exactly experts.
    - They are self-authoring, have a sense of responsibility regarding Circles 1-6, consciousness regarding Circles 7-8, and an understanding of their own professional domain but no particular knowledge about the other six and are unable to connect them.
    - During a pandemic curfew, they become more and more terrified as they realize how few people are washing their hands.

Most people would probably prefer to live in the first community or nation-state, and if we were to invest our money somewhere, we would probably put our money in the first society as well.

A Rose Garden Society

What would our lives, our societies, the world, and our economies for that matter, look like if we created a bildung society and a bildung economy? Or a 'Rose Garden Society' where all individuals, all institutions, organizations and companies, and society as a whole were considered "Roses" where the seven domains needed to be in balance? Where all seven domains were more or less equally supported and funded? Or if that were the goal, at least?

It is easy to misunderstand this rose garden analogy as a totalitarian state where all roses are pruned to boredom in strictly defined rose beds, but that is not the idea. The idea is to create the best soil and growing conditions for everybody, so that everybody can grow to become the rose they have the potential to be. And the image of the garden holds a double quality of both nature and cultivation.

A Rose Garden Economy

Bildung is not a question of money per se, but at the societal level, education and bildung throughout the population is a question of where society allocates its financial resources. Likewise, the economy is also a question about bildung: is the population educated and does it have the bildung to create a stable economy, and what is prioritized when legislation defines the rules for our economic activities?

Part of today's necessary bildung in order to create a sustainable economy is the understanding that consumption of natural resources, i.e., production of trash, cannot keep growing exponentially on a finite planet. As economist, educator and philosopher, Kenneth E. Boulding (1910-1993) expressed it:

> Anyone who believes that exponential growth can go on forever
> in a finite world is either a madman or an economist.

What *can* go on forever, are self-organizing, open, complex eco-systems, i.e., nature. Today, we understand our economies as growing systems that need to produce interest on debt (in effect, exponentially). Instead, we can understand economies as eco-systems that must be self-sustainable and long-term. Economies also must be full of life and initiative, in inner balance, and functioning in harmony with nature and its eco-systems. Once we understand that, we ought to be able to create a sustainable economic model. That model will be as different from both the current capitalist growth model and from the communist economy, as capitalism and communism are from the feudal economy they replaced. (If you are an economist or political scientist reading this and thinking, "THE ECONOMY CANNOT WORK WITHOUT GROWTH!!!", you are right: the *current* economy cannot work without growth. That is why we need to rethink it.

Nobody knows what a self-sustainable bildung eco-economy might look like, but given the fact that restarting the old economy after the corona lockdown is going to be a problem anyway – if for no other reason, then because globalization must be fundamentally reconsidered due to considerations regarding security and supply chains – maybe considering a different model would be in place.

The current economic, capitalist model is really good at solving one problem: turning limited resources into material wealth and trash. It does so by factoring in capital and labor but ignoring the consumption of land and energy, and by rewarding those who are willing to risk their own capital for the opportunity to be rewarded with more capital later. The capitalist model takes natural resources, including energy, and turns them into exponentially increasing amounts of consumer goods while increasing the amount of capital and trash accordingly. The capitalist model itself cannot distribute the capital in the system in such a way that everybody can keep consuming, only political intervention can secure that. The capitalist model left to its own devices has a trickle-up-effect, where the people with the most capital will keep sucking up the capital that is created, hence the name Monopoly of the game Monopoly. Tellingly, that is a game that just dies out as soon as everybody can tell who the winner is going to be; has anybody actually ever cared to play it to the end? Capitalist economies without political will to redistribute capital work just like that.

The eco-economic Rose Garden model, which is so far just a sketch of an idea, is somehow structured around regenerative cycles that allow everybody to keep contributing, learning, teaching, being involved, creative, productive, and engaging in producing meaningful goods and services that do not increase the production of trash. A greater proportion of the consumption is immaterial and more stuff is recycled or upcycled, and this is factored in as a measurement in the economic model.

In nature, there is no money, no jobs, but there is plenty of work and exchange, and the 'legal tender' are water, oxygen, and carbon dioxide. Every organism in an eco-system participates in the constant exchange of those three substances; every organism is both a consumer and a producer. Overall, plants take up carbon dioxide and produce oxygen, animals take up oxygen and produce carbon dioxide, and all organism circulate water.

In an eco-economy where we are all considered "Roses" that need to thrive, the measure of success is the extent to which everybody is both a producer and a consumer in the same legal tender. But contrary to the capitalist, the communist, and the feudal economies, legal tender is not just a currency recognized by the financial system. Since we are animals, we circulate water, we take up oxygen and produce carbon dioxide, and since we are humans, we take up spirit, reproduce it and with bildung, we give it our personal expression through work. Since we live in complex imagined communities, we circulate capital in order to make exchanges of work and natural resources feasible. A long-time sustainable economic model would ensure a balanced circulation of natural resources, ideas/spirit, and money in and among all seven domains and among all Circles of Belonging. The question is how we unite their sustainable balance with an economy that needs to keep growing as long as we have unpaid debt with interest. Can the corona lockdown be an existential escape door to a different economic model? Do we have the imagination to envision that and the bildung to dare pursue it?

The one thing that can keep growing in any society and its economy is our inner world, our spirit, the quality of our work, our meaning-making, our sense of responsibility, and our character and uniqueness in interplay with our surroundings. Our bildung. Including the bildung that allows us to integrate into society and the economy, those who are still newcomers to the world and who cannot compete. In the capitalist economy, those who are beginners, who learn slow, who cannot keep a job on market terms, who perceive the world differently, who are clumsy, and who cannot compete and perhaps not even collaborate, are excluded from the production side of the economy and are marginalized on the consumption side. Competition, rather than collaboration, defines the old economy, and people are excluded if they cannot compete. A bildung Rose Garden eco-economy that values collaboration and bildung over competition, that does not use more natural resources than it returns, and that measures its success on the extent to which everybody is both a producer and consumer, can actually grow exponentially. Not in energy consumption and production of trash but in inner richness, in meaning-making, in collaboration, and in moral character, perhaps particularly among the most competitive. Competition is good for some purposes, but it has to be fair, and there has to be a level playing field for all. A bildung eco-economy could be the kind of culture and economy that can embrace, contain and even enjoy diversity; the odd, the deviant, and the lesser abled will still be unique, their perspective and contribution will always be different, a challenge and a pushback to some. A culture, economy, and civilization that values the people with the most challenges for the pushbacks they offer the rest of us will also be humanity and civilization at their best. The corona lockdown has already shown that global civilization cares more about the vulnerable than about the market.

A garden is both nature and culture: we have taken plants from nature, organized them according to our own needs and imagination, and cultivated them. Our cultivation can be more or less in harmony with the rest of nature. We can use the mechanisms already present in nature and 'capture software,' to get a 'free ride' on processes already out there, such as using certain bugs to fight weeds or other bugs, and using manure from animals as fertilizers. Alternatively, we can use chemicals as pesticides and fertilizers. The first method does not produce as high a yield as the second. Instead, if done right, the first method can go on forever like nature itself because it *is* nature itself. At some point, artificial pesticides and fertilizers affect the surrounding nature in unwanted ways, such as killing off the pollinators or polluting the water.

We need to find the right balance between nature and culture, both with regards to how we produce our food and how the human animal is an integral part of the organic circles of life on our planet. The economic model that we set up as the defining infrastructure of our inter-human exchanges of nature's gifts and our own inventions and activities, must be in harmony with the rest of the planet, with nature.

What I mean by a Rose Garden Economy is an economic model, where each individual Rose, i.e. each individual human being, each family, each community, each country, each continent, and the globe as a whole are seen as Bildung Roses within Bildung Roses, and where the seven domains of each of these Roses, at all levels of complexity, must be in balance and thrive.

Since this is a garden, it is both nature and culture, and we are the gardeners. Each one of us as individuals and each family, community, nation, continent, and the global community through the many transnational institutions are Roses and gardens. The good gardener cares about the entire garden, not just a corner. The good gardener knows the cycles of the local climate, reads nature, and adjusts the garden. The good gardener plans years ahead, cares about the future of both soil, water, fungi, animals, and plants, and is careful about sun and shade for each rose to grow and flourish the most.

If we go beyond the image of the rose garden, gardening as such is an interesting human phenomenon. It was the earliest form of human manipulation of nature; it came before settled agriculture and animal husbandry. There is also something telling about the size of a garden: if it is too small, it is just a patch of soil, a backyard; if it is too big, it is a park or a market garden. Gardens have a human scale. How do we know that? We just do. There is something inherently human about gardens that make them feel like gardens. I guess what defines it is that one or two adults can tend a garden and keep it flourishing, and it can feed a family.

Across the most stress-, anxiety- and depression-ridden parts of the world, gardening is becoming a tool for healing. Giving in to the pace of nature and watching things grow soothes our soul. Watering, pruning, picking weeds, fertilizing, planning, digging, planting anew, and looking forward to flowers and harvests and homegrown meals makes us happy, makes us flourish. Something deep inside us connects, and we ourselves are cultivated, along with the garden.

Across the same stress-, anxiety-, depression-, and not least loneliness-ridden parts of the world, gardening is also being rediscovered as a way for local communities to flourish, as a way of improving the environment and as a way of reducing food transportation and waste. Neighborhood gardens, rooftop gardens, backyard gardens, all kinds of gardens are appearing in cities and are bringing humans, nature, and our own inner nature together. As the great wheel of time drives the changes of the seasons, there are springs and harvests, constant change and unfolding of life, and a rhythm that connects us to that from which we came and tells us to surrender to nature, and that is bildung too. Human spirit. Ruach. Atman. Geist.

It is perhaps significant that the Danish folk-bildung and folk-highschool movement were so intimately connected to agriculture. Improving the production of food at a time when starvation was normal must have been deeply meaningful on its own. Connecting this meaningful work to the larger picture of developing one's country and serving a higher purpose must have been a truly awesome feeling; even shoveling manure suddenly got a deeper meaning.

Today, in the West, we are not physically hungry and materially deprived; we die from overeating and overconsumption. Globally, obesity is a bigger problem than hunger. Instead, our starvation is of the spirit, and for that, we need bildung.

Whatever we make out of the corona lockdown and of the rest of the 21st century is a choice. Nothing is predestined, it is in our hands. Nothing stops us from doing exactly what we did before the pandemic. Nothing stops us from choosing differently; choosing differently just requires new kinds of education, new bildung, new conversations, new knowledge and new ideas.

What do we choose and how do we choose to do it?

Sources

Abbt, Thomas: *Vom Tode für das Vaterland* (1761)

Abbt, Thomas: *Vom Verdienste* (1765)

Adams, Frank with Myles Horton: *Unearthing Seeds of Fire: The Idea of Highlander* (John F. Blair, 1975)

Adler, Hans and Wulf Köpke: *A Companion to the Works of Johann Gottfried Herder* (Camden House, 2009) Agarth, Carl Adoph: *Reservation mot Stora undervisningskommitténs slutbetänkande* (1828) from Burman, Anders and Per Sundgren: *Bildning* (Daidalos, 2010)

Almqvist, Carl Jonas Love: *Det går an* (Det går an, Danish translation: Ida Jessen, Gyldendal, 2008)

Alsheimer, Leif: *Bildningsresan – Från ensidig instrumentell utbildning till sammanhangsskapande bildning* (Bokförlaget Prisma, 2004)

Andersen, Lene: *Globalt gearskift* (Det Andersenske Forlag, 2014)

Andersen, Lene Rachel og Björkman, Tomas: *The Nordic Secret -- A European Story of Beauty and freedom* (Fri Tanke, 2017)

Andersen, Lene Rachel: *Metamodernity* (Nordic Bildung, 2019)

Andersen, Lene Rachel: *The Bildung Rose* (Nordic Bildung, 2019)
http://nordicbildung.org/publication/the-bildung-rose/

Andersen, Poul E.: *Det myteløse menneske* (Aschehoug, 1969)

Austlid, Andreas: *Ein folkelærar* (Gyldendalske Boghandel, Nordisk Forlag, 1911)

Bairoch, Paul: *Europe's Gross National Product: 1800-1975,*: (1976)

Beutin, Wolfgang and Klaus Ehlert, Wolfgang Emmerich, Helmut Hoffacker, Bernd Lutz, Volker Meid, Ralf Schnell, Peter Stein, Inge Stephan: *A History of German Literature: From the Beginnings to the Present Day* (Routledge, 2005)

Bjørn, Claus: Folkehøjskolen og Andelsbevægelsen (Selskabet for skole- og uddannelseshistorie, Årbog 1971)

Bjørnson, Bjørnstjerne: *En Hanske* (1883)

Björkman, Tomas: The Market Myth (Fri Tanke, 2016)

Björkman, Tomas: Världen vi skapar (Fri Tanke, 2017)

Booth, Michael: *The Almost Nearly Perfect People* (Vintage Books, 2015)

Bradley, S.A.J.: *N.F.S. Grundtvig a Life Recalled* (Aarhus University Press, 2008)

Brandes, Georg: *Samlede skrifter 1-13* (Collected writings 1-13) (Gyldendal, 1919)

Branting, Hjalmar: Op-ed (Arbetet, 10 August, 1889)

Brinkmann, Svend: *Stå fast – et opgør med tidens udviklingstrang* (Gyldendal Business, 2014)

Bruford, W.H.: *The German Tradition of Self-Cultivation – 'Bildung' from Humboldt to Thomas Mann* (Cambridge University Press, 1975)

Brühlmeier, Arthur: *J.H.Pestalozzi – Auswahlt aus seinen Schriften Vol. 1-3* (Uni Taschenbücher, 1979)

Brühlmeier, Arthur: *Menschen Bilden* (Verlag Merker im Effingerhof)

Brühlmeier, Arthur: *Head, Heart and Hand – Education in the Spririt of Pestalozzi* (Sophia Books, 2010)

Bruun, Kristoffer: *Folkelige Grundtanker* (For Kirke-, Skole- og Folkeoplysning – Tillæg til Oplandenes Avis, No. 6, 1877, 1 Årgang)

Bruun, Christopher: *Folkelige Grundtanker* (Alb. Cammermeyers Forlag, 1878)

Bukdahl, Jørgen and Jens Marinus Jensen (editors): *Fri Ungdom – Dansk folkeligt Ungdomsarbejde* (Forlaget Arnkrone, 1944)

Burman, Anders and Per Sundgren: *Bildning* (Daidalos, 2010)

Burman, Anders and Per Sundgren: *Svenska Bildningstraditioner* (Daidalos, 2012)

Bygdén, Leonard: Benjamin Höijer. En kort sammanställning af hans lefnad och filosofiska tillstånd (J. Sundvallson, 1782)

Christensen, Dan. Ch.: *Hans Christian Ørsted – Reading Nature's Mind* (Oxford University Press, 2013)

Danske Frimurerorden, Den: *I Guld og Himmelblåt – Frimureriet i Danmark gennem 250 år – 1743-1993* (Den Danske Frimurerorden, 1992)

Duetoft, Peter: *Frimureri – fortid eller fremtid?* (Den Danske Frimurerorden, 2003)

Eigaard, Søren (editor): *Velfærd og folkeoplysning* (Odense Universitetsforlag, 2002)

Eckermann, Johann Peter: *Samtaler med Goethe* (Gespräche mit Goethe, excerpts translated by Elsa Gress, Hans Reitzels Forlag, 1963)

Engberg, Hanne: *Historien om Christen Kold, en skolehistorisk afhandling* (Gyldendal, 1985)

Evangelisk Kyrkovän, various issues 1854-1857.

Federlin, Wilhelm-Ludwig: *Von der Güte des Herzens und dem Wohlwollen – Die vorzüglichen Seelen-kräfte in der Philosophie Thomas Abbts* (Journal of Religious Culture, Journal für Religions-kultur, no. 111, 2008)

Fibiger, Mathilde: *Clara Raphael Tolv Breve* (1851) (Lindhardt & Ringhof, 1976)

Fichte, Johann Gottlieb: *Beitrag zur Berichtigung der Urteile des Publikums über die französische Revolution* (1793)

Fichte, Johann Gottlieb: *Tal till tyska nationen* (Albert Bonniers förlag, 1914)

Fichte, Johann Gottlieb: *Über den Begriff der Wissenschaftslehre* (Reclam, 1972)

Fichte, Johann Gottlieb: *Die Bestimmung des Menschen*, (Der Vossischen Buchhandlung, 1800 / Reclam, 1962)

Fiell, Charlotte and Peter: *Scandinavian Design* (Taschen, 2002)

Frisch, Hartvig: *Europas kulturhistorie* (Politikens Forlag, 1962)

Fromm, Erich: *Escape from Freedom* (1941) (Avon Books, 1965)

Geijer, Erik Gustaf: *Försök till en kort översikt av uppfostran, dess särskilda arter och dessas förhål-lande till staten* (1826) from Burman, Anders and Per Sundgren: *Bildning* (Daidalos, 2010)

GEO EPOCHE Nr. 52: *Otto von Bismarck*

Gilroy, Paul: *The Black Atlantic* (Verso Books, 1993)

Goethe, Johann Wolfgang: *Götz von Berlichingen mit der eisernen Hand* (1773)

Goethe, Johann Wolfgang: *Die Leiden des jungen Werter* (1774)

Goethe, Johann Wolfgang: *The Sorrows of Young Werther:*

Goethe, Johann Wolfgang von: *Briefwechsel zwischen Schiller und Goethe, Vol. 1* (1805)

Goethe, Johann Wolfgang von: *Faust* (in Danish translation – version can currently not be veri-fied)

Graff, Harvey J. et.al.: *Literacy and social development in the West*, (Cambridge University Press, 1981)

Graves, Clare W.: *Human Nature Prepares for a Momentous Leap* (The Futurist, April 1974)

Green, Allan: *Kierkegaard bland samtida* (Förlags AB Gondolin, 1995)

Grundtvig, Nikolai Frederik Severin: *Smaaskrifter om den historiske Høiskole* (Karl Schønberg, 1872)

N.F.S. Grundtvigs Bibliothek (N.F.S. Grundtvig's Library) Catalogue of the books from Grundtvig's library that were put up for sale in 1873 after his death (see image below)

Gur-Ze'ev, Ilan: Diasporic Philosophy and Counter-Education (Sense Publishers, 2010)

Gärdenfors, Peter: *Tankens vindlar* (Nya Doxa, 2005)

Gärdenfors, Peter: *Den meningssökande människan* (The meaning seeking human), (Natur och Kultur, 2006)

Gärdenfors, Peter: *Lusten att förstå* (Natur & Kultur, 2010)

Haidt, Jonathan: *The Righteous Mind* (Vintage Books, 2012)

Hall, John A., Ove Korsgaard, and Ove K. Pedersen: *Building the Nation – N.F.S. Grundtvig and Danish National Identity* (Djøf Publishing, 2015)

Hammerich, Paul: *Lysmageren : en krønike om Poul Henningsen* (Gyldendal, 1986)

Hansen, Jan-Erik Ebbestad: *Norsk tro og tanke 1800-1940, vol. 2* (Tano-Aschehoug, 1998)

Hastedt, Heiner: *Was ist Bildung* (Reclam, 2012)

Heafford, M.R.: Pestalozzi: *His Thought and its Relevance Today* (Routledge, 2016)

Hegel, G.W.F.: *Phänomenologie des Geistes* (1807 / Reclam, 2014)

Hegel, G.W.F.: *Åndens fænomenologi* (Gyldendal, 2005)

Hegel: De Store Tænkere; Uddrag af diverse tekster (excerpts from various texts – Danish trans-lation Oskar Borgman Hansen, Rosinante, 2000)

Henningsen, Poul: *Kulturkritik Bind I-IV* (Rhodos, 1973)

Hentig, Hartmut von: *Bildung* (Karl Hanser Verlag, 1996)

Herder, Johann Gottfried: *Journal meiner Reise im Jahr 1769*

Herder, Johann Gottfried: *Auch eine Philosophie der Geschichte zur Bildung der Menschheit* (1774)

Herder, Johann Gottfried von: *Sammtliche Werke: zur Philosophie ..., Volume 16*

Hertel, Hans: *Det stadig moderne gennembrud* (Gyldendal, 2004)

Holmberg, Teodor: *Den svenska folkhögskolan* (Föreningen Heimdals Folkskrifter. — N:r 45. – F. & G. Beijers Bokförlagsaktiebolag, 1897)

Horton, Myles with Judith Kohl & Herbert Kohl: *The Long Haul, an autobiography* (Teachers College Press, 1998)

Humboldt, Wilhelm von: *Ideen zum einem Versuch, die Grenzen der Wirksamkeit des Staats zu bestimmen* (Reclam, 1967 / 2005)

Hume, David: *An Enquiry Concerning Human Understanding* (1748)

Høiris, Ole and Thomas Ledet (editors): *Romantikkens verden – Natur, menneske, samfund, kunst og kultur* (Aarhus Universitetsforlag, 2008)

Høverstad, Torstein: *Ole Vig – Ein norrøn uppsedar* (Forlag Norrøn Livskunst, 1953)

Ibsen, Henrik: *Et Dukkehjem* (1879)

Ibsen, Henrik: *En Folkefiende* (1882)

Ignasiak, Detlef: *Das Literarische Jena* (Qvartus Verlag, 2012)

ILO: Global Estimates of Modern Slavery (2017)

Jacob, Margaret C.: *Living the Enlightenment – Freemasonry and Politics in Eighteenth-Century Europe* (Oxford University Press, 1991)

Kant, Immanuel: *Zum ewigen Frieden und andere Schriften* (Fischer Taschenbuch Verlag, 2008)

Kant, Immanuel: *What is Enlightenment?*

Kant, Immanuel: Uddrag af *Kritik af den rene fornuft* samt *Grundlæggelse af moralens metafysik* (excerpts from *Kritik der reinen Vernunft* and *Grundlegnung zur Metaphysik der Sitten* – Danish translation Justus Harnack; from De store tænkere, Rosinante, 1991)

Kegan, Robert: *The Evolving Self: Problem and Process in Human Development* (Harvard Univeristy Press, 1982)

Kegan, Robert: *In Over Our Heads: Mental Demands of Modern Life* (Harvard University Press, 1994)

Kegan, Robert: *Immunity to Change: How to Overcome It and Unlock the Potential in Yourself and Your Organization* (Leadership for the Common Good) (Harvard Business School Publishing Corporation, 2009)

Kemp, Peter: *Løgnen om dannelse – opgør med halvdannelsen* (Tiderne Skifter, 2015)

Kemp, Peter: *Verdensborgeren – Pædagogisk og politisk ideal for det 21. århundrede* (Hans Reitzels Forlag, 2013)

Keßler, Martin: *Johann Gottfried Herder – der Theologe unter den Klassikern: Das Amt des Generalsuperintendenten von Sachsen-Weimar* (Walter de Gruyter, 2007)

Key, Ellen: *Bildning. Några synpunkter* (1897) from Burman, Anders and Per Sundgren: *Bildning* (Daidalos, 2010)

Key, Ellen: *Från människosläktets barndom* (Studentföreningen Verdandis Småskrifter, 1888)

Key, Ellen: *Moralens utveckling*, 1891 Fri bearbetning efter Ch. Letourneau: *»L'Évolution de la morale»* (Studentföreningen Verdandis Småskrifter, 1891)

Key, Ellen: *Individualism och socialism* (Studentföreningen Verdandis Småskrifter, year unclear)

Key, Ellen: *Skönhet för alla* (Studentföreningen Verdandis Småskrifter, 1870 / 1891 / 1904)

Kierkegaard, Søren: *Enten-Eller* (Either-Or) *Vol. 1 & 2*, 1843 (Samlede Værker vol. 2 & 3, Gyldendal, 1962)

Kierkegaard, Søren: *Stadier på Livets Vei* (Stages on Life's Way) Vol. 1 & 2, 1845 (Samlede Værker vol. 2 & 3, Gyldendal, 1962)

Knudsen, Jørgen: *Georg Brandes – den mangfoldige* (Gyldendal, 2005)

Koch, G.H. von: *Om Arbetarnas Konsumptionsföreningar i England* (Studentföreningen Verdandis Småskrifter, 78, 1899)

Kold, Christen: *Tale ved Vennemødet i København 1866.*

Koller, Hans-Christoph: *Bildung anders denken – Einführung in die Theorie transformatorischer Bildungsprozesse* (Kohlhammer, 2012)

Korsgaard, Ove: *A Foray into Folk High School Ideology* (FFD (the folk-high-school association in Denmark), 2019)

Kühn, Manfred: *Johann Gottlieb Fichte: Ein deutscher Philosoph* (C.H. Beck, 2012)

Laloux, Frederic: *Reinventing Organizations* (Nelson Parker, 2016)

Lambert, David A.: *How Repentance Became Biblical – Judaism, Christianity, and the Interpretation of Scripture* (Oxford University Press, 2016)

Laneth, Pia Fris: *1915 Da kvinder og tyende blev borgere* (Gyldendal, 2015)

Larsen, Christian, Erik Nørr og Pernille Sonne: *Da skolen tog form 1780-1850* (Aarhus Universitetsforlag, 2013)

Lausten, Martin Schwarz: Kirkehistorie – grundtræk af Vestens kirkehistorie fra begyndelsen til nutiden (Anis, 1998)

Lessing, Gotthold Ephraim: *Nathan der Weise* (1779)

Lessing, Gotthold Ephraim: Die Erziehung des Menschengeschlechts (Gotthold Ephraim Lessing, 1780)

Liessmann, Konrad Paul: *Theorie der Unbildung* (Piper Verlag, 2008 / 2015)

Lindeman, Eduard: *The meaning of adult education* (New Public, Inc., 1926)

Linge, Karl: *Hur den svenska folkskolan kom till* (Studentföreningen Verdandis Småskrifter, no. 62, 1911)

Lübcke, Poul: *Politikens Filosofileksikon* (Politikens Forlag, 1995)

Maddison Project, The: Bolt, J. and J. L. van Zanden (2014). *The Maddison Project: collaborative research on historical national accounts.* The Economic History Review, 67 (3): 627–651 (2913)

Marx, Karl: De Store Tænkere; Uddrag af diverse tekster (excerpts from various texts – Danish translation Johannes Witt-Hansen, Rosinante, 2000)

Mendelssohn, Moses: *Über die Frage: was heißt aufklären?* (1784)

Merle, Jean-Christoph (ed.): *Johann Gottlieb Fichte: Grundlage des Naturrechts* (De Gruyter, 2016)

Mezirow, Jack, Edward W. Taylor, and Associates: *Transformative Learning in Practice – Insights from Community, Workplace, and Higher Education* (Jossey-Bass, 2009)

Michelsen, Wilhelm: *Pædagogik og livssyn* (Selskabet for Dansk Skolehistorie: Årbog for dansk skolehistorie, 1967, p.48-58)

Mykland, Knut: *Norges Historie, Bind 11 To kulturer en stat 1851-1884* (J.W. Cappelens Forlag, 1976-80)

Nealon, Jeffrey T.: *Post-Postmodernism or, The Cultural Logic of Just-in-Time Capitalism* (Stanford University Press, 2012)

Nida-Rümelin, Julian: *Auf dem Weg in eine neue deutsche Bildungskatastrofe – Zwölf unangenehme Wahrheiten* (Verlag Herder, 2015)

Nida-Rümelin, Julian: *Der Akademisierungswahn – Zur Krise beruflicher und akademischer Bildung* (Körber-Stiftung, 2014)

Nida-Rümelin, Julian: *Philosophie einer humanen Bildung* (Körber-Stiftung, 2013)

Nielsen, Anton: *Om Hans, der kom paa Høiskolen* (O. H. Delbanco, 1867)

Nielsen, Anton: *Om Karen, der kom paa Høiskolen* (O. H. Delbanco, 1868)

Nielsen, Niels Kayser: *Bonde, stat og hjem* (Aarhus Universitetsforlag, 2009)

Nietzsche, Friedrich: *Antikrist* (Der Antichrist. Flucht aus das Christentum – Danish translation by Peter Thielst, Det lille Forlag, 2005)

Nietzsche, Friedrich: *Således talte Zarathustra* (Also sprach Zarathustra – Danish translation by Niels Henningsen, Det lille Forlag, 1999)

Nietzsche, Friedrich: *Menneskeligt, alt for menneskeligt* (Menschliches, Allzumenschliches – Danish translation by Niels Henningsen, Det lille Forlag, 2007)

Olsson, Oscar: *Folklig självuppfostran* (1918) from: Burman, Anders and Per Sundgren: *Bildning* (Daidalos, 2010)

Pestalozzi, Johann H.: *Sämtliche Werke und Briefe. Registerband 1*

Pestalozzi, Johann Heinrich: *Meine Nachforschungen über den Gang der Natur in der Entwicklung des Menschengeschlechts*

Piaget, Jean: *The Language and Thought of the Child* (Routledge Classics, 2001)

Piaget, Jean: *Psychology Of The Child* (Basic Books, 1969, 1971, 2000)

Pilling, Claudia; Diana Schilling, Miriam Springer: *Friedrich Schiller* (Rowolt Taschenbuch Verlag, 2002, 2010)

Pirtle, Wayne G.: *German Adult Education Following the Unification of 1871* (Adult Education, 23, 2, 99-114, W 73)

Rauhut, Franz, Ilse Schaarschmidt, Wolfgang Klafki: *Beiträge zur Geschichte des Bildungsbegriffs* (Verlag Julius Beltz, 1965)

Rousseau, Jean-Jacques: *Discourse on the Arts and Sciences*

Rousseau, Jean-Jacques: *Emile*

Rousseau, Jean-Jacques: *Considerations on the Government of Poland*

Rousseau, Jean-Jacques: *Julie, or the New Heloise*

Rousseau, Jean-Jacques: *The Social Contract*

Rousseau, Jean-Jacques: *Emile vol. 1*

Rousseau, Jean-Jacques: *Emile vol. 2*

Rousseau, Jean-Jacques: *Discours sur les Sciences et les Arts* (1750)

Safranski, Rüdiger: *Goethe – Kunstwerk des Lebens* (Fischer Taschenbuch, 2015)

Safranski, Rüdiger: *Schiller – oder Die Erfindung des Deutschen Idealismus* (Hanser, München 2004)

Safranski: Rüdiger: *Goethe und Schiller. Geschichte einer Freundschaft* (Hanser, München 2009)

Scavenius, Bente: *The Golden Age Revisited – Art and Culture in Denmark 1800-1850* (Gyldendal, 1996)

Schaarschmidt, Ilse: *Der Bedeutungswandel der Worte "bilden" und "Bildung" in der Literaturepoche von Gottsched bis Herder*, in: *Beiträge zur Geschichte des Bildungsbegriffs*, (as reproduced in Beitrage zur Geschichte des Bildungsbegriffs, Verlag Julius Beltz, 1965)

Schanz, Hans-Jørgen: *Frihed* (Aarhus Universitetsforlag, 2012)

Schelling, F.W.J.: *Über das Wesen der menschlichen Freiheit* (Reclam, 1964)

Schiller, Friedrich: *Die Räuber* (1781) (Reclam, 1969, 2014)

Schiller, Friedrich: *Die Räuber* (1781)

Schiller, Friedrich: *Über die ästhetische Erziehung des Menschen, in einer Reihe von Briefen* (1795)

Schiller, Friedrich: *On the Aesthetic Education of Man* (Penguin Classics, 2016)

Schiller, Friedrich: *On the Aesthetic Education of Man* (Dover Publications, 2004)

Schück, H., K. Warburg: *Illustrerad Svensk Litteraturhistoria* (Hugo Gebers Förlag, 1929)

Schück, Henrik: Allmän Litteraturhistoria (Hugo Gerbers Förlag)

Seitter, Wolfgang: *Geschichte der Erwachsenenbildung* (Das Deutsche Institut für Erwachsenenbildung (DIE), 2007)

Shaftesbury, Anthony Ashley-Cooper, 3rd Earl of: Volume 1: (1707-27)

Shaftesbury, Anthony Ashley-Cooper, 3rd Earl of: Volume 2: (1707-27)

Shaftesbury, Anthony Ashley-Cooper, 3rd Earl of: Volume 3, (1707-27)

Simon, Erica: – *og solen står med bonden op – De nordiske folkehøjskolers idehistorie* (Askov Højskoles Forlag, 1989)

Skovmand, Roar: *Samspillet mellem Nordens folkehøjskoler indtil Anden Verdenskrig.* (Universitetsforlaget i Aarhus, 1983 / Jysk Selskab for Historie, 41, 1983.)

Snellman, Johan Vilhelm: *Om det akademiska studium* (1840) from Burman, Anders and Per Sundgren: *Bildning* (Daidalos, 2010)

Sohlman, August: *Om bonde-högskolor. : Förhandlingar i Nordiska nationalföreningen den 5 och 11 dec. 1867.* (Aftonbladet, 1868 / National Library of Sweden)

Spicer, Chriss (editor): *Lifted by the Heart – Writings from Option, Journal of the Folk Education Association of America* (Circumstantial Productions, 2009)

Staaff, Karl: *Församlingsrätten*, (Studentföreningen Verdandis Småskrifter, 1891)

Stephenson, George M.: *The Religious Aspects of Swedish Immigration* (The University of Minesota Press, 1932)

Stewart, Jon: *Kierkegaard and His Contemporaries: The Culture of Golden Age Denmark* (Walter de Gruyter, 2003)

Strindberg, August: *Röda rummet* (1879)

Strindberg, August: *Nya riket* (1882)

Suny, Ronald Grigor and Michael D. Kennedy: *Intellectuals and the Articulation of the Nation* (University of Michigan Press, 2001)

Svenning, Olle: *Hövdingen. Hjalmar Branting: En biografi* (Albert Bonniers Förlag, 2014)

Sørensen, Svend and Niels Nielsen: *I hælene på Christen Kold – En skildring af en thybo og hans skole* (Sparekassen Thy's Forlag, 1990)

Taylor, Edward W., Patricia Cranton and Associates: *The Handbook of Transformative Leraning – Theory, Research, and Practice* (Jossey-Bass, 2012)

Tegnér, Esaias: *Tal i Jönköping skola* (1827) from Burman, Anders and Per Sundgren: *Bildning* (Daidalos, 2010)

Theml, Christine: *Schiller und Goethe in Jena* (Verlag Janos Stekovics, 2009)

Tøsse, Sigvart: *Folkeopplysning og vaksenopplæring, idear og framvekst gjennom 200 år* (Didakta Norsk Forlag, 2005)

University of Aarhus: about the Danish slave trade:
https://danmarkshistorien.dk/leksikon-og-kilder/vis/materiale/ernst-schimmelmanns-brev-af-18-juni-1791-om-slavehandelen/
https://danmarkshistorien.dk/leksikon-og-kilder/vis/materiale/forordning-om-negerhandelen-1792/

Vieweg, Klaus and Michael Winkler: *Bildung und Freiheit – Ein vergessener Zusammenhang* (Ferdinand Schöningh, 2012)

Vig, Ole et al.: *Folkevennen* (periodical, Selskabet til Folkeoplysningens Fremme, years 1852, 1853, 1854)

Similar periodicals from the same time:

Fattig og Riig, et Søndagsblad til opbyggelig Underholdning (H. Halling, personel Kapellan, 1848-49, M.C. Fabritius's Bogtrykkeri)

Almuevennen (weekly periodical, 5 issuse 1849)

Maanedstidende for den norske Almueskole – Under medvirken af norsk Kirketidendes Redaktør, Cand. i Theol. Th. C. Bernhoft med flere Theologer og Lærere (B.S. Krognæss, Skolelærer i Aker, 1861, B.M. Bentzens Bogtrykkeri)

Vygotsky, Lev: Mind in Society, Harvard, 1978

Welzel, Christian: Freedom Rising: *Human Empowerment And The Quest For Emancipation* (Cambridge University Press, 2014)

Wäktaren, Tidning för Stat och Kyrka, 17 January 1855.

Wäktaren, Tidning för Stat och Kyrka, 20 January 1855.